AGAINST ALL ODDS

By

Theresa Hiney Tinggal

I use the word *'adopted'* loosely hence the inverted commas throughout the book, in order to make the story simpler for the reader. I, however, was never adopted but (secretly) illegally registered as the biological child of the Hiney's, therefore, people whose births were illegally registered do not identify as adopted people, as no legal adoption ever took place. Other people were adopted through adoption agencies and subsequently registered as their biological child. Both methods, however, were illegal.

I have changed the names of my biological family, whom I discovered in Tipperary through DNA in 2017, at their request.

The address of Nurse Doody's house, 85 Collins Ave, was, in fact, 84. Very often, names were added incorrectly.

Dedication

Dedicated to my mother, Alice Monica (Mona)

4th August 1922–31st August 2009

Sadly, she passed away before we met.

I searched for you for 16 years and would have searched forever.

The statute of heartbroken mother and child on the back cover signifies the lifelong grief suffered by both mother and child.

The Memorial for Unborn Children by Martin Hudacek © 2010

The front cover is me as a 4yr old child in Dublin 1958. The red coat represents lost innocence and the deliberate ignorance of those who were of aware of 'child trafficking' in Ireland.

About the Author

This is the true story of a woman who, at the age of 48, discovered that her parents were not her birth parents. It is the story of her subsequent sixteen-year struggle to uncover the truth and find her true family.

Brought up in Ireland, Theresa Tinggal moved to England at the age of 19. Subsequently marrying, she had two children, Tara and Ryan. She loves being a grandparent to Mia and Ruby, visiting them regularly in Australia. Having discovered at the age of 48 that James and Kathleen Hiney were not her biological parents, she was on a mission to establish the truth and has campaigned relentlessly over the past 20yrs in Ireland for an investigation into illegal adoptions/registrations. This all came to fruition, however, when in March 2022, the Irish government published a report into illegal registrations opening the door for adoptees, both legal and illegal, to access their birth files. Her motto, *'If no one speaks up, nothing changes,'* has carried her through, against all the odds over the last 20 years, culminating in the discovery of her biological family in Tipperary, Ireland, in 2017 through DNA. She has had a varied career, is now semi-retired, and living in Bournemouth, England. This is her first book.

Life changed forever by illegal adoption in Ireland.

If nobody speaks up, nothing changes,

Theresa Tinggal

Table of Contents

Acknowledgements

I extend my heartfelt thanks to so many people who have helped me on my journey to find my identity. Your support has been so appreciated and very humbling.

Conall O'Fatharta, a former journalist at the *Irish Examiner*, whose passion for justice and his constant and consistent reporting of illegal registrations and illegal adoptions kept this issue in the spotlight.

I will be eternally grateful to Sharon Lawless (Flawless Films), the producer of *Adoption Stories*. Their research team spent hundreds of hours trawling through my DNA results and eventually unearthing my biological family in Co Tipperary.

I want to thank Dr. Maurice Gleeson, the DNA genealogist, for all his help and support in advancing my knowledge of DNA testing. Also, Terri Harrison, for all her love and support, even though she has not been reunited with her beloved son, Niall. Without hesitation, Kevin Battle, one of the Banished Babies, allowed me to use his story.

Maura Griffin, illegally registered, managed to find her mother through DNA testing. Mary Harris (not her real name), whose illegal adoption, like mine, was arranged by Nurse Doody. Pauline Bonfield for her valuable insight and encouragement.

So many people have kept firmly believing in what I was doing over the years. I am grateful for their unfailing support and encouragement as they came with me on this unbelievable journey. There are too many to list by name, but one person who stands out is Susan Burgess-Lock, a friend for more years than I can remember. She has always been at the other end of the phone and never hesitated to help me with my IT problems—and there were many!

i

From the beginning of my journey, my children have been an emotional bulwark: my daughter Tara, my beloved grandchildren Mia and Ruby (who, understandably, can't fathom how this could have happened and thankfully have never had to live in such a repressive era) and my son Ryan. During my journey, I often sought my son's opinion, and he, now a man in his 40s, finds the whole story incredible as it is! My children are a living, breathing affirmation of a mother's love for her child. Finally, over the years, there have been many people who have told me their stories. There have been many who have suffered terribly, so this book is for all of you.

Foreword

(Conall O'Fatharta, Journalist)

21 February 2023

It's been ten years since I first picked up a phone to hear the voice of Theresa Tinggal on the line. In many ways, everything has changed in the decade since that first call. Yet nothing has. The previously largely disinterested public has become an increasingly vocal and a key ally of the now adult victims of coerced, illegal adoption and their mothers who spent decades living in the shadows: silent and forgotten. And yet they wait for basic rights that the rest of us take for granted - access to birth certificates—basic information on their early lives. The rights for it have existed in other countries for decades. It is largely thanks to Theresa that these issues have now made headlines both nationally and internationally. At a time when forced and illegal adoption remained a subject just whispered about, she put forward her own experience as a living testimony. We can't know how many others she has inspired to speak out, but we can be sure she has been an inspiration to countless people.

Theresa was forty-eight when she discovered that the people she knew as Mam and Dad were not her birth parents. They had been given two-day-old Theresa and registered her as their natural child some six weeks later—a more criminal offense than it is now. It was a secret kept by her family for the best of half a century and kept secret by the Irish State. The same state that, astonishingly, monitored her progress for the first sixteen years of her life, keeping a detailed file on her. Having had her identity taken from her without her consent, Theresa was determined to find who she was and help others find their identities. If that meant pouring her heart and soul into a young reporter, so be it. She described her sorrow when reading that file—her life through someone else's eyes.

Reading the file relating to me was the weirdest thing I have ever experienced. Details about me at school, going to work, what I looked like. I felt that I was dead and reading my life story. I can't really put it into words, but it was like I was reading about someone else and felt my whole life was a lie. Sometimes I still can't believe that all this has happened. In the following pages, Theresa rights that lie. This is her truth: her life, through her eyes.

The Language of Fairy Tales

Sharon Lawless, author/producer of Adoption Stories

The language of fairy tales is often used in the world of adoption. Birth parents are envisaged as princes and princesses who arrive in a blaze of festivities to break the spell of wicked witches who stole their children. They are beautiful, young, and in love. Their lives are complete, and they all live happily ever after. Unfortunately, the reality is more Grimm than Disney.

I first met Theresa at Heathrow Airport before she boarded a flight for her annual visit to her daughter, Tara, and her daughter's family in Australia. I had flown over to meet Theresa to see if she would agree to be filmed on her search for a woman who officially didn't exist—her mother. Theresa's story was so unbelievable that I couldn't convince the main broadcaster and the film board that it was true and needed to be exposed. Surely it couldn't be that high profile? Surely, it couldn't be that those in respected medical, legal, political, and religious networks privately colluded to traffic babies? These were dynasties, household names, and powerful, influential, and successful people. But they did. And they had got away with it, again and again.

I won't spoil what's ahead of you in this book. It contains Theresa's incredible tale of secrets, lies, corruption, and injustice and her relentless campaign to expose it; however, I will give you a brief history lesson to explain how Theresa's story came to need telling. Theresa will expand the details in the following pages, but this is what happened.

Ireland wasn't always a land of saints and scholars, as its current reputation would have us believe. In the early twentieth century, the Irish Republic began to rise after eight hundred years of oppression by the English. The Free State was established in 1922, and Irish people could again be their people. From then until 1937, society was somewhat permissive, with people now free from the shackles of foreign rule and being downtrodden. People started to have careers, build prosperity, socialize, and celebrate—and then Eamon de Valera, an ultra-conservative politician, became Taoiseach. He aligned himself with the powerful Archbishop John McQuaid, and between them, they locked Ireland into a Church/State partnership that still exists: the then financially decimated government would look after rebuilding the country. In contrast, the Church looked after the social aspects—hospitals, schools, and institutions.

Women were suppressed, contraception was made illegal, and almost anything joyous was frowned upon, if not deemed a sin. These two men concerted efforts to ensure Ireland was a white, Catholic-controlled, and blemish-free country. Sex before marriage was a big no-no; even worse was the evidence of sex before marriage, which was pregnancy. Women in this condition were ostracised and families shamed, resulting in thousands of women and children having no choice but to go into the now infamous mother and baby homes. Here they paid for their 'sin' financially through arduous and relentless work and having their babies taken for 'adoption'. The law introduced in 1952 to legalize adoption still means neither the natural parent nor the relinquished child has the right to know anything about each other.

A married couple who did not produce children was almost as big a no-no. It was an insult to the Church not to 'go forth and multiply; in a male-dominated society, it was seen as a failure for a man to be impotent. Not every couple who wanted to adopt conformed to the legal criteria, though, so a gap in the market opened. The export of white Catholic babies to childless white Catholic couples in the U.S.A. had worked exceptionally well. A similar scheme within the country could be just as lucrative.

High-profile and well-connected medical, legal, political, and religious personnel formed networks to avail of the predicament of unmarried women who wanted to hide their pregnancies and the married couples deemed unsuitable to be parents. Private nursing homes were common at the time, and married women often gave birth in these, rather than a maternity hospital. What better places to accommodate unmarried pregnant women where records weren't examined as thoroughly as in a public hospital? Usually, a big house in an affluent area was converted. There was plenty of space to keep unmarried women from the 'respectable' clientele. The pregnant woman was referred by a social worker, doctor, priest, or another well-connected family friend. She was assured her pregnancy would be covered up, so no future employer or husband would ever know she was 'damaged goods. A fee was paid for her time in the home, and she was spared the insults and back-breaking work common in the mother and baby homes. Her time was her own. She could read, write and even send letters detailing the great cuisine or secretarial course she was supposedly on for six months.

In the meantime, a couple who could not pass the Health Board examination to be considered suitable adoptive parents made it known to their doctor, priest, or some other well-connected party, that they wanted a child of their own. The reasons for being turned down officially included advanced years, alcoholism, mental health issues, or violence. The reason didn't matter to the networks—as long as the prospective parents could pay the fee, they passed with flying colours.

The baby was handed over to the adoptive parents within days of birth, who were instructed to register the child as their own. The midwife would organize the baptism with the adoptive parents named the natural parents. Even the private nursing home's own register had no record of the woman who had given birth, so there was no trace of any illegitimate baby in her name. Nobody would ever know. Except everyone knew. All the people involved, many who were household names, signed off on the births, made the arrangements—and made fortunes. This practice lasted for at least twenty-five years, and in all that time, not one person was ever charged and convicted. The corruption, greed, and disregard for women and children are still evident in legislation and in the reluctance of those affected to entertain legal action.

Theresa's narrative is a raw, honest description of her experience at finding out about her illegal adoption and her search for her true identity. It is also an exposé of these illegal activities and who should be held accountable. This book describes how this strong, determined woman took on the authorities to get the justice she and thousands of others deserve.

I will tell my children that I did not stay silent!

When you are illegally adopted/registered, there is no proof that you exist. A doctor's signature is absent from your falsified birth certificate because there was never a birth officially. Your birth certificate is a fabrication and is null and void. Useless. You are proving nothing; hence, you can never find where you came from or belong. This is cruelty beyond belief. You started life as a lie, and you lived your life in limbo—forever looking for that something that is missing—your identity.

Orphaned /1954

What years have passed, and shadows cast

On a person's right to know
Their parents that had sown the seed
To make this baby grow

What rights have they in following years
To lock it all away
And keep these secrets from the child
Until the present day.

And even now the lips are sealed
And documents amiss
The cruelty of adoption
Is like a Judas kiss.

So, to fight for right to find the name
For those children in the past
Some self-imposed office fool
Will make their torment last.

And those people with the right to know
Their years will slip away
Unless the records are released
To give them peace of mind today.

By

Tony Gorman

INTRODUCTION

The most traumatic experience of my life occurred in 2002 when I discovered that my birth certificate was false at the age of forty-eight, and I was not the daughter of James and Kathleen Hiney[1]. I presumed this was my unique experience, but when I began my research, I realized that thousands were like me. Thousands who, too, have no idea they are not who they think they are or knowledge of their true identity. There are thousands whom the Irish government has chosen to ignore. Under the Ireland of Cardinal McQuaid and President de Valera, facilitated by the Catholic Church, thousands of mothers were coerced into giving up their babies. These babies were given to 'good Catholic families' for a generous sum. The unfortunate young mothers were not helped or supported but were shunned by society for the 'sin' of having a baby out of wedlock. Terri Harrison, the mother of Niall, shares her story experience.

Try to imagine or remember the feeling when you discover you will become a mother for the first time. You wonder about the little person you are going to give life to. What sort of mother will you be? There is all the anxiety that surrounds this very new invasion of your own body. The fear of responsibility. The fear of something going wrong. There are all the questions you want answers to. The reassurances that your unborn baby is safe.

You look forward to loving your new-born baby boy or girl. It does not matter which. All that matters is that you do your best throughout your pregnancy to take good care of yourself both—rest, stay calm and get all the right nutrients to ensure your unborn grows

---

[1] In this book, my adoptive parents, James and Kathleen Hiney, will be identified by their first names.

1

strong and healthy inside you. And so, your bond with your unborn grows. You feel the kicks, the slow movements, and you hope.

This is what most new expectant mothers go through. They get the best medical care possible, attend prenatal classes, and learn breathing techniques. They prepare for the most miraculous moment of their lives: a time that will stay with them for the rest of their lives— the birth of their child.

So why was this not true for thousands of expectant mums, mums who could never have imagined the fate that awaited them? The fear of being left to die or their unborn baby would not be looked after, so they may never be allowed to mother their own child because they would be deemed unfit to be their own child.

My son was born in an institution called St Patrick's in Navan Road, Dublin. In 1973, I escaped to the UK, but like most young women in my situation, I was alone and unsupported and an easy target for those who wished to arrange 'adoptions' for our unborn babies. I was targeted and taken back to Ireland by the Catholic Crusade and Rescue Society, a well-known, well-established religious group with its main office in London and branches in other parts of the UK. Each branch was connected to all the various institutions in Ireland, and the organisation was directly involved with adopting babies, legal and otherwise. In Ireland, I was put into a mother-and-baby home.

It is hard to imagine the world young women occupy in these homes. It was a hostile world where young, healthy women, who happened to be pregnant, were hidden away. She couldn't keep her baby, although many tried. As did I. Many always hoped that help would come, that someone would stop the cruelty. But the large, locked doors admitted neither a familiar face nor loving arms to save them and their baby. The titles they gave included 'unmarried mother', 'biological mother', and 'birth mother'. Like many other teenage girls, I was never acknowledged as a 'mum; on the contrary, we were mostly treated as non-human. Within the walls of most of these institutions (they were called 'homes' but were far from offering the warmth of homes), every girl was identified by a new house name and number.

Despite their pregnancy being at an advanced stage, they were made to do hard physical work with limited time to rest and with no care or concern being shown to them or their unborn child. If they showed signs of ill health, they were told to pray, ask their God for forgiveness, and ask him to spare them and their child. Sadly, the prayers of many of these young women were never answered. Some lost their own lives. Others gave birth but were told their baby had died and they had to continue working. They could not leave until those in charge deemed fit to return to society.

I would like to introduce you to Mona, who, as a young woman, shared my experience of being part of a society that viewed us as 'criminals'. Our crime? Was it giving birth—life—to our babies? As criminals, the sentence we received was loss (what I have termed our 'living bereavement'), which would last a lifetime.

Mona's (my mother) experience is mirrored in the pages of this book. She understood that society had turned its back on her and her baby. There was no way she could know what became of her baby. There was no way she could know what the future had in store for her baby. Above all, her baby would never know his/her mother's name—that it is Mona.

This book accounts for my journey, which I, Theresa, never thought I would have to take. I am writing to tell the world what happened in Catholic Ireland from the 1950s to the 1970s. More importantly, I want to describe the devastating effect on those who suffered under what I consider a cruel regime—the Catholic Church.

Even now, I sometimes ask, *God did this happen to me?* Time and time again, I've asked myself, *why? Why did this have to happen to me at the age of forty-eight?*

It is my conviction that everyone is put on earth for a reason. I now have my answer to the *Why?* It is to expose the truth and shine a light on what has been hidden for far too long, that is, finding out the truth about my identity at the age of forty-eight (perhaps much later than normal to discover you are not who you thought you were) prompted me to reveal the illegal adoptions of babies in Ireland that became a very lucrative industry. Nowadays, the practice would be identified as child trafficking.

I was not the only one affected. There are thousands of us. I hope that by sharing my personal experience, people will have a greater understanding of what it is like for us and that more people will have the courage to speak out and be *silent no more*.

PART 1: MY STORY

Chapter 1
My Early Life

Theresa Marion Hiney: 9 June 1954–15 May 2002

I was that person!

I did not die on 15 May 2002. At least not in the physical sense. That day, I discovered I was not Theresa Hiney, who had grown up in Rathfarnham, Co. Dublin. That was the day my identity, as I had known it, was shattered into a thousand pieces. That was when I found out I had been lied to by my family for forty-eight years. That was the day my uncle told me, '… "*they are not your parents*". As I stood in my kitchen in Bournemouth, my world was spinning. I kept thinking, *what on earth do you mean, Uncle Pat? They must be my parents. My birth certificate says they are.*

"I don't know how they did it, Theresa, but I was over on holiday from England, and there you were, a small baby, playing on the floor", my uncle told me. Your father told me that they had adopted you, *but* he continued *"not in the legal sense"* My uncle told me that he hadn't enquired any further because questions were never asked in the 1950s, and with much shrouded in secrecy, it was easy to keep such things hidden. As my uncle and I talked that fateful day, I was reminded of when I was growing up, and the many times' people had said, 'You look nothing like your family' or 'Theresa is the odd one out. I didn't share their talents. For example, I wasn't musical like other members of the family. *I now knew that I was indeed the odd one out.*

Rathfarnham, where I had lived from the age of six months, is a suburban area on the south side of Dublin, nestling at the foot of the Dublin mountains. In the 1950s, it was still a little village out in the country, and we were rather isolated. No one in the neighbourhood had cars, and the bus routes were limited. The women in the housing estate at the top of Nutgrove Avenue, where we lived, had a long walk to the closest shops—an arduous task with small children in tow.

On some Saturdays, Bernie and I would board the double-decker 16a bus with Kathleen and head off to 'town', as we referred to Dublin, for a day's shopping and, before we headed home, our special treat in the Woolworths restaurant. We loved the bustle of Dublin and hearing all the street vendors with their broad Dublin accents, but the bus trip was the most fun. Because buses were the main transport, the bus was always crowded, and I often had to stand in the aisle so that adults could have the seats. Unlike today there were no mobile phones, so people talked to one another, and we could rely on a comedian on the bus whose jokes we didn't understand. We nevertheless joined in the collective hilarity. There were also philosophers discussing the state of the world and others discussing local politics, sports, or the rising cost of living.

I did not have any concept of time on these bus trips, and I recall looking out the window at the river Dodder as the bus chugged along through Terenure, Harold's Cross, and George's Street, occasionally stopping to let people off. An abiding memory is of driving past the iconic Yellow House pub, the heart of Rathfarnham. The pub was built in 1825, but it is believed that the original Yellow House pub was a quaint, early French Gothic-style thatched cottage dating from the eighteenth century and situated on the site of the present Church of the Annunciation.[2] The pub gave way to the Church of the Good Shepherd, Churchtown, which opened its doors in 1957 to accommodate the now sprawling parish. The blessing of the new Church was carried out by none other than Dr. John Charles McQuaid, the Archbishop of Dublin, who was known for the unusual

[2] 9https://www.archiseek.com/2009/1878-new-catholic-church-rathfarnham-co-dublin

amount of influence and unacceptable level of sway over the Irish government.

In later years, on my way home from Dublin airport, I always felt great joy when I passed these familiar places. I especially loved seeing the Dublin mountains, which appeared suddenly out of nowhere, displaying various shades of green, like an artist's easel. I knew, at last, I was home!

The mountains form a large part of my childhood memories. James (my father, as I then believed) took us out every Sunday for walks in the mountains. These walks in the fresh air weren't expensive–an important consideration when finances were tight. The mountains also always remind me of Christmas Eve. James would come down the passage to our bedroom excitedly shouting, "I've just seen Santa Clause and his reindeer coming down the mountain. You had better be asleep!" With our eyes tightly shut and pretending to be asleep, Bernie and I would cling to each other, afraid to even breathe for fear that Santa's elves may be peeping in the window. These are

Rathfarnham Village

8

happy memories, and I have continued the Christmas Eve tradition with my children and grandchildren–*sans* the glorious mountains!

I have two sisters: Margaret and Bernie. Margaret, James and Kathleen's natural daughter, was five years old when I joined the family as her sister, a two-day-old baby. She describes her memories:

For those of us who have been fortunate enough to enjoy a happy start to life, childhood recollections are some of the most cherished memories we have. Somehow, almost miraculously, wafts of the distant past weave a shadowy recreation of events of long ago. Perhaps it is God's little way of preserving those treasured moments by implanting them in our minds. Who knows?

*Having been born and brought up in the suburbs of dear old Dublin in the 1950s and 60s, I enjoy a treasure trove of memories from a time that was so different from today's world. For instance, in the 1950s, cars were as rare as a man walking on the moon in Cabra, an inner suburb on the north side of Dublin where we lived when I was five. It was quiet enough that a motor car would have been exceptionally uncommon to pull up outside your house. Indeed, such an event would inevitably arouse neighbours' curiosity down the road, with them declaring, 'Janey Mac, there's a terrible big vehicle pulled up outside Jimmy Hiney's house!' It would certainly have kept the 'chattering classes' of Carnlough Road entertained for weeks. However, during one particular week, two – yes, **two** – motor cars pulled up outside the Hiney abode. What could this mean? One of the vehicles was owned by Mrs. Hannan, the wife of a Dublin judge, no less. The other, which pulled up some days later, belonged to a budding politician in the form of Tom Byrne. Mr. Byrne was the son of Alfie Byrne, who enjoyed several terms–ten, in fact–as the Lord Mayor of Dublin. He also served as a TD in Dáil Éireann.*

The straight-talking Mrs. Hannan wanted to discuss the possibility of child adoption with my parents. Looking back now, I realize it was quite clearly a furtive, even clandestine, rendezvous: cloak and dagger, some might say. To me, a young, innocent five-year-old, it felt more of an intriguing, exciting occurrence. When the indomitable Mrs. Hannan asked me if I would like a new baby brother or sister, unsurprisingly, my reply was in the affirmative. What excitement! Tom Byrne's visit some days later was quite unconnected, and its purpose was to recruit my father as an election campaign worker. At the tender age of five, I was introduced to the world of politics.

Some days after the 'royal' visit, a telegram arrived, it caused my mother serious distress, and she would not open it, fearing that it was either bad news concerning her brother Pat, who lived in England, or that the planned 'adoption' had fallen through. My poor mum, a perpetual worrier, was in a dreadful state of anxiety until my dad eventually arrived home from work and opened the telegram. It was merely a request from Tom Byrne to place election boarding in front of our house! My mother roared, 'Tom Byrne and his feckin' poster!' I had never heard my mother swear before nor, to be honest, ever have since. The three of us stood, shocked. She was patently traumatized.

Fortunately, Mammy's anxiety was soon relieved when news arrived that a bundle of joy would soon be amongst us. When the day arrived, I was ushered next door to stay with the Donnelley's while Mam went to fetch the baby. Mrs. Donnelly, who I referred to as 'Don-Don', was a kindly soul, and I had been a regular visitor to her house for as long as I could remember. The day passed in excited anticipation, and I suddenly had a baby sister. It was a very happy day at that house in the inner-city suburb of the northside of Dublin when Theresa arrived at Carnlough Road in Cabra.

When the excitement and novelty of the new arrival had abated, I discovered, much to my surprise, that I had gained less of an instant playmate and more of a dependant whose only activity seemed to be sleeping, crying, and feeding. It was a salutary lesson for me, the older sister! Then the big day arrived when infant Theresa was introduced to solids. A rusk was gently dipped into a dish of warm milk, and most important of all, the sign of the cross was made over it. I blinked in astonishment as Mammy performed this strange ritual. Would my baby sister survive the trauma? I earnestly believed that the sooner Theresa took to the solids, the sooner she would grow up and be able to play with me. Maybe Mammy would have been better feeding her on colcannon, I speculated.

Bernie, who is two years younger than me, had been fostered. The failed uprising against communist rule in Hungary in 1956 led to an influx of refugees. Ireland had joined the UN only weeks before, and its High Commission for Refugees requested that Ireland take a quota of these refugees, with acceptance representing a badge of membership of the UN 'club'. The figure of 571 was agreed upon, and the refugees were warmly welcomed. In Ireland, there was the perception that because the refugees were Catholics who communists had driven out, they were one of us. Among the refugees were some mere infants who needed to be fostered.[3]

We loved the story my mother used to tell us at bedtime—how when she went to choose a Hungarian baby, she saw Bernie and, being captivated by her big blue eyes, promptly brought her home! She made it sound as if it had been that easy. Although the circumstances were not quite as my mother described, the story certainly wasn't too

[3] Steve O'Brien. Hungarian refugee crisis presented Ireland with a new challenge. https://www.unhcr.org/en-ie/news/latest/2006/11/454f3a95a/hungarian-refugee-crisis-presented-ireland-new-challenge.html

far from the truth. Kathleen had been approached once again by Mrs. Hannan, and again, Kathleen's contact was Mareece Hannan.

Bernie was fostered by the Health Board (HSE, now Tusla), who kept an eye on her until she was 16. She had been born on 11 November 1956 but only came into our family on 25 January 1957 as gastroenteritis had kept her in St Ultan's children's hospital for over two months. My dad brought her home for what was supposed to be a trial weekend and never took her back! No official check-up on her for several months. The HSE escaped having to pay the stipulated fostering allowance for Bernie to my parents by saying she had been privately fostered. (Yes—but the arrangement had not been with her birth mother!) Bernie was always aware that she had been fostered, but it did not really seem to bother her. I was delighted when she joined the family, as the five-year gap between Margaret and me meant that we seldom played together. Bernie and I were always linked; I would have been very lonely without her.

I later discovered that we had moved from Cabra to Rathfarnham because people in the community were curious and started asking questions about me and the circumstances of my 'adoption'. James

James and Kathleen Hiney who brought me up.

12

and Kathleen decided to make a fresh start where this would remain a fiercely guarded secret. However, James (who could never be found in the vicinity of diplomacy) trustingly revealed the secret to a neighbour. In no time, the whole neighbourhood was aware of my status. I was the only one who remained oblivious. I was the only one unaware I that I was not a Hiney up until the age of 48!

Me age 22 – still unaware I wasn't who I thought I was

My childhood was never boring, and our home was full of fun when James was not away in England searching for work. He had many attributes, being clever, politically astute, and a great entertainer. I loved the times we had with relatives in our home when James would sneak upstairs to dress in Kathleen's clothes and recite one of his funny monologues to rapturous applause and laughter. This was made even funnier because James was a slight man, and Kathleen was a large woman. He was well known as a composer of ballads and, with his incredible ability to play by ear, was always popular at parties. It was not unusual for musicians to congregate in our home after a night out. My sisters and I each had a little piece to perform at parties. As a four-year-old, I would recite *A song for dad* and continue with a rendering of *Brahm's Lullaby*, especially for James—never Kathleen, interestingly enough. I have no idea how I learned it at that tender age! Ironically one of my other party pieces was *Nobody's Child*. I also spent many afternoons at the Abbey Theatre in Dublin, having tagged along to rehearsals of plays with James, and I am very grateful to have been introduced to my Irish culture during these times.

Margaret remembers: *When Theresa was a toddler, she had an imaginary friend called Paddy. The structure of our home in Rathfarnham offered plenty of unhindered space for her to manoeuvre her doll's pushchair at pace. Finishing at the front of the house, she would take great care to park the pushchair before putting on a headscarf precisely and then announcing, 'Can ye smell the prayers, Paddy?' She was at church, and as she got older, Theresa became a very confident 'pushchair aficionado'. She would wander near and far on many an exploit, once having to be brought home by one of the guards from the local garda barracks in Butterfield Avenue. This was perhaps an early indication of her interest in travel, which was to become a part of her future life.*

I remember clearly my first day at school when James took me to Our Lady of Loreto Convent as a four-year-old. I was late for my very first class! My primary school days were not happy; I have no memories of any kindness shown by the nuns, only of feeling terrified. (I wonder if cruelty is a vocational prerequisite for a nun. At least for the nuns who ran the schools, but that same cruel streak was evident to thousands of incarcerated single mothers in mother and baby homes.) I remember the missionary nuns who visited our school from time to time were kind. They were like a breath of fresh air, and we were lucky to have them as teachers. Perhaps their kindness was because they were more in tune with life and doing what they loved: helping on the missions and setting up schools without any of the luxuries available in the convents.

I did very well at school, but by the end of my junior phase, I had had enough of the nuns, and I refused to continue my secondary schooling at the convent. Instead, I went to The Institute of Tailoring and Textiles in Parnell Square in Dublin to fulfil my dream of being a dress designer. The difference between the two schools was unimaginable, and looking back, I can honestly say that my years there were the happiest of my young life. We had only lay teachers (no cruel nuns), and I was treated as a person with potential, being encouraged in all my endeavours. Best of all, much to my surprise, there was no physical punishment. I continued to excel at school, and the pride my father showed in me was sometimes embarrassing. When I got a Saturday job a couple of doors away from where he worked, he used to bring his own customers to see me, saying, *'Look, that's my Tess. Isn't she lovely?'*

We had a happy childhood, but there were difficult times as well. James' strong principles cost him his job with Dublin Corporation when he publicly addressed union representatives denouncing communist infiltration at City Hall in 1956. Not long after, he refused to take the job of a man in prison for being in the IRA. It was their chance to eliminate this man they saw as inciting unrest. While he was unemployed, James did not receive one penny of aid, and our family suffered financially to the point where I did not have sufficient warm clothing. One day, in desperation, James and Kathleen took Bernie and me to the Social Services office in the city. I clearly remember the dull brown décor and the desperation on people's faces—men, shrouded in smoke, were bent forward, no doubt wondering how they would feed their families. It was a day I will always remember for more than one reason. * *

Leaving us there, James and Kathleen walked out. They had discussed this with us, and had told us they would be back after ten minutes, but watching my parents walk out, leaving me in that depressing office, was too much for me. All hell broke loose, and I howled the place down. People had to leave the office, and I remember a lady giving me a glass of milk, trying to calm me down. Despite this, no offer was made to help my parents, not even the bus fare home, and we were a sorry sight as we walked from Dublin to Rathfarnham. Looking back, I am astounded by the lack of compassion shown to us that day. ** research has shown that another reason I was taken there was that my mother, Alice Monica, tried to take me back. If only she had been successful, but because of the illegalities that were involved not just with the Hineys' but also the authorities, a huge scandal of illegal adoptions and registrations would have unfolded. Because of this, I was deprived forever of being with my mother.

As a young child, I had a very close relationship with James and seemed to need to be in close physical proximity to him. When he was at home, I stuck to him like glue, and he would have to sneak out of the house to go to work if I was around. One of my earliest memories is of me at two years old, running after him as he left the house, my blonde curls bobbing up and down. I would sob for hours after he had gone. The same occurred when James was working in England. I would get so upset when he left that he didn't warn me he would be leaving, disappearing from my life and leaving me distraught. I remember coming downstairs one morning to find James lighting the fire. He had unexpectedly arrived home from England, but I was so shocked that I just stood and stared at him and didn't say a word for hours.

Unlike my relationship with James, my relationship with Kathleen was always strained, and I think I unnerved her somewhat. From a young age, I constantly stood and stared at her, almost as though I sensed something was wrong. James used to say, *'Theresa, don't stare at your mother like that',* probably aware of the onslaught that would follow when he was not around. It did not take much for her to unleash her temper on me! I was a serious child, rarely smiling except when my father was around. I must have sensed her lack of love. I certainly sensed that her treatment of Bernie and me differed from how she treated Margaret, her natural daughter, who she put on a pedestal. *'Why can't you be more like Margaret?'* was her constant mantra. Bittersweet words now that I know the truth. Certainly ironic! I could never understand why Kathleen was so cold toward me. As described earlier, Margaret remembers me heading off with my dolls. My memories are of me running away in an attempt to get attention or as a cry for help. I had no idea where I hoped to go, and I never went far–maybe a mile–before I turned back. Often, I would look furtively behind me and see James following at a distance.

I have a clear memory of how the atmosphere changed in our home on an occasion when Kathleen was admitted to the hospital. We were allowed to play outside with the other children, and my father would be singing away. I remember feeling guilty about thinking how nice it would be if it were just us and James in the home. My uncle

Pat, with whom I have always had a close relationship, told me that over the years, it had pained him when I talked about my lack of a warm relationship with Kathleen, especially when I compared this with my relationship with my two children. They have always meant the world to me.

As the years passed, even after I had moved to England, Kathleen's attitude continued to be a source of distress. I had never felt the unconditional love children are supposed to receive from their mothers, and I had even begun to discuss my pain with a friend. Perhaps somewhat intuitively, I had recently confided in her that it felt like I had not come from Kathleen's body. At one stage, I contemplated booking a flight to Dublin to ask Kathleen why she had treated me as she had. Perhaps fate was preparing me for the revelation and for the journey I would embark on as a consequence of my discovery.

Reflections on my Childhood

Until the age of 48, my memories of my childhood and family life were intact, and the narrative was undisturbed. But in an instant, the narrative was distorted. I look back and reflect on my childhood through a different lens.

I have often wondered how it was that I never knew I had been adopted, but I think when we were younger, if adoption was discussed at all, we probably had quite a romantic view of it. In our family, it was a secret not to be discussed. Bernie never asked about her mother. She seemed to accept her situation, and I concluded that she did not have to suffer the trauma and deceit of finding out that her life had been one big lie. It was the lies that were my problem, not the fact that I had been illegally registered as their biological child.

Although my birth certificate declared I was the child of James and Kathleen, I think somewhere deep in my psyche, I knew something was not quite right. With my child's limited cognitive ability, I could not make sense of what was wrong but now, having discovered the truth about my 'adoption', the pieces of the puzzle have fallen into place, and I can understand what I could not as a young child. I now know that my mixed and confused feelings during my childhood were a yearning for a mother's love. I understand now that there was no bond between Kathleen and me. I used to break down and cry with my closest friends who had loving, warm mothers. I so missed having what they had, while at the same time, I felt guilty that I didn't love Kathleen as I loved James. I know, without a doubt, that I was loved unconditionally by James. Had Kathleen been able to love me with the same unconditional love I so desperately needed as a child, perhaps I would not have had such an empty space in my heart throughout my life.

Looking back, I remember that throughout my childhood, people constantly pointed out that Bernie and I looked nothing like each other. Despite knowing, I never once explained the reason for this. I never told anyone that we were not sisters. As far as I was concerned, she was my sister. Even my own children did not know until my own situation revealed that we were not biological sisters. From my perspective, I don't understand why adoptive parents need to announce their adopted child's status. Surely this child, who is a gift and has completed the family, should be regarded as their own?

Admission to their adoption can contribute to an adoptee struggling with their identity and constantly asking, 'Who am I'? Adoptees may be struggling with the emotional trauma of their own mothers, perhaps not wanting them. Constant reminders of their adoption compound these feelings. How can they ever feel part of a family that is not biologically theirs? The feelings of rejection are twofold. Kathleen had told me my situation was a secret, but it wasn't. Both my sisters, relatives including my uncle, our neighbours in Rathfarnham, and Margaret's four children in England, knew about it. Why did they need to know but not me? I was not to know. I was invisible. It could almost be described as harnessing the power within the family, the power vested in the secret holder rather than the content. 'I have a secret. I want other people to know that I have been the privileged owner of that secret for a long time before I divulge it to you. You are now part of that privilege—our little secret club.

I know that my experience is not the experience of all adoptees, and there are probably many people who could give glowing reports of their adoption experience. I also realize that I was probably lucky as the alternative to being 'adopted' would have been to spend my childhood in an orphanage and attend an industrial school. (That, however, does not make it right!) Some mothers do not form a close bond with their natural child, and the child senses a lack of love. When I was older, on one of my trips home, I suggested to Kathleen that sometimes even natural mothers cannot bond with their child, but Kathleen would not hear of it. She needed to be perceived as a perfect mother, and admitting liability would have been too difficult.

I always thought I was at fault, but I had come to believe that Kathleen's attitude had less to do with me and more with a family affair that occurred before I became part of the Hiney family. In the 1950s, if a mother died suddenly, her children were temporarily cared for by neighbours and other family members. When this happened to a local mother of eleven children, my parents took in six-month-old Barry and instantly fell in love with this cherubic, smiling baby. I can understand why. We grew up with a picture of Barry on the sideboard, and I can still see his chubby little face and blonde curls. However, regularly and after spending nights in the pub, Barry's dad would call at our house. Eventually, my father decided enough was enough when

Barry's father became abusive. Barry was returned to his father (with, unfortunately, a poor outcome for Barry and his twin brother in their later years). Kathleen was devastated, and I am sure she never got over losing Barry. I am sure James thought my 'adoption' would fill the gap, but I could never replace Barry in her life. It is no wonder that she found it difficult to bond with me. How different my life and Barry's would have been if he had stayed with the Hineys and another family had fostered me. In hindsight, my father's efforts to help Kathleen, who may have had more general mental health problems, were probably as effective as sticking plaster on a deep wound. It didn't work.

Chapter 2
Who Am I?

Reeling from my uncle's disclosure, I phoned Margaret, who was living in England. As I blurted out, 'I've just been told I was adopted, I was convinced she would tell me that it wasn't true, that Pat was getting old, that he had it all wrong. To my horror, I heard her saying, "Oh my God! Who told you?"

"Yes, I've always known," she answered.

'And Bernie?'

"Yes. Mam told her when she was sixteen. You must be devastated", was Margaret's reply.

Standing with the telephone in my hand, rooted to the spot for what seemed like hours, I felt destroyed. On the outside, I still looked like me, Theresa, but inside I didn't know who I was anymore. In time, I managed to order my thoughts, knowing that but for my uncle's disclosure, I still would be none the wiser. I would have spent the rest of my life believing that my mother, Kathleen, didn't love me.

I could not believe that I had been allowed to live a lie every day of my life because it suited those involved. It seems ironic that the one thing we got clattered for in our house was lying! What double standards! I had never guessed the truth, but my birth certificate showed James and Kathleen as my parents, so why would I question this? However, everything fell into place. I now knew why I had always felt like the odd one out, not fitting into the family. From an early age, I had known deep down that Kathleen, and I did not have a normal mother-child relationship. Now I knew that we did not share one iota of DNA. All I could think of and my reply to Margaret was, *'to be honest, I am so glad to find out that I am not related to that woman'*. In fact, I felt elated that there was no biological connection between Kathleen and myself.

I also experienced an intense feeling of exclusion. All the members of my family, as well as my community, knew I had been 'adopted'. Even the State, which knew of my illegal registration, had kept it a secret from me. I was the only one who didn't know. I was shattered to discover that people I had trusted would betray me like this. It seems this deception was permitted as it suited the agenda of others. I felt that I was a commodity, being used for the well-being of others. The well-being of Kathleen was considered, with no thought ever given to how it would affect me.

To clarify and make sense of this horrendous revelation. I went to see Kathleen to ascertain the truth about who I was, visiting her three or four times that year. I believe she had written down her version as she never deviated from the story, repeating it word for word. On my first visit, she appeared restrained as she descended the stairs, straightening the collar on her cardigan. Kathleen was a tall, well-built woman who could be intimidating. Unlike my father, she seldom showed her emotions, so it took me years to interpret her body language. Now she seemed tense while lowering herself into a comfortable armchair before revealing how I came into their lives.

I Join the Family

According to Kathleen, James was in the city one day when he met an old friend holding a little girl's hand. While exchanging pleasantries, James commented, *'I didn't realize that you had an addition to the family'*.

'Well, we got her, but not in a legal way' was the reply: the same words used to explain my presence to Pat not too many months later.

(I wonder how often this had been the reply to similar questions and how often the same dialogue had been repeated in hushed tones. Probably thousands.) James then admitted to his friend that he and Kathleen would have loved to have more children, but there were problems with this. The friend indicated that he could help in this regard and took James' contact details.

Some months later, a chauffeur-driven car pulled up outside our house in Cabra, as described by Margaret. What Margaret did not mention was that the visitor, Mrs. Hannan, and her husband, Mr. Justice Hannan, were the parents of Mareece Hannan, the almoner of the Coombe Hospital, Dublin. Mrs. Hannan opened the conversation by saying that she had been made aware of James and Kathleen's desire to have a child and then told my mother about an unmarried woman whose baby was due in June. To the question of whether she would be interested in taking the baby, Kathleen readily replied in the affirmative. The visit concluded with Mrs. Hannan telling Kathleen that she would be contacted when the baby's arrival was imminent. It was as simple as that—an exchange like any other.

Kathleen was duly contacted on 9 June 1954, the day I was born. However, I am still unsure where I was born, as she and James went to collect me from Nurse Doody's house in Collins Avenue, Dublin, on 11th June. Nurse Doody accompanied James and Kathleen to the local church, Our Lady of Consolation, Donnycarney, where I was baptized as Theresa Marion Hiney. It was a Thursday afternoon, not a normal day for baptisms, and I was the only infant baptized that day. I do not doubt that the priest knew exactly what was going on and that the whole process was well rehearsed.

That Thursday was a wonderful day for one family, as a new baby was welcomed into their home. It was marked by unimaginable trauma for two people: mine at being separated from my mother, and my mother's, who had to go back to Tipperary and continue as though nothing had happened. She would have had some comfort in knowing that I would be with loving parents, as she believed.

The Health Board Becomes Involved

Two years passed, during which my presence in the Hiney household had escaped the notice of the authorities. This changed, however, when Kathleen decided that she would like to foster a child. Another child? She could hardly cope with the ones she had! This seemed to be a surprising decision, considering I was still a toddler. In hindsight, I surmise that Kathleen enjoyed babies but not a stubborn two-year-old who challenged and outstared her.

When Kathleen and James approached the Health Board about fostering a child, questions were asked about me. Now the Health Board knew about my 'adoption' and began monitoring my progress. An inspector's report on my file from November 1956 confirms knowledge of my illegal adoption.

Mrs. Hiney admits that she took this child of two days from Mrs. Doody of Collins Avenue. She also admits that she got £45 from Mrs. Doody towards maintaining the infant. Mrs. Hiney states that she had the baby baptized and the infant's birth registered in both her and her husband's name. In other words, the child's birth is registered as the legitimate daughter of Mr. and Mrs. Hiney.

Despite the Health Board having this information, there was never an investigation into those involved. At the time, there was no more than a half-hearted attempt to find my biological mother. Two months after a social worker had asked, 'I would respectfully ask the board for a direction in this case in January 1957, the social workers recorded what appears to have been the only effort made to find my natural mother:

I called to 85 Collins Avenue, both east and west, and have failed to trace a Mrs. Doody. I have also failed to find the mother of this child.

My Perceptions

Even though a social worker checked up on me for fourteen years, I don't recall ever being asked how I felt. I was never asked 'how things were' or how I got on with my siblings. Neither was I ever asked how I got on with Kathleen and James. My family was poor, and my mother suffered from depression. Being just a child, I guess I would have said everything was ok, although I knew deep down that there were problems. Why was I allowed to continue living in that home under those circumstances? My biological mother would have assumed I was going to a family where I would have had better opportunities and the very least, loved.

I firmly believe there was a coordinated cover-up effort to protect the professionals involved. It seems impossible that the authorities were unaware of Nurse Doody, particularly, as she was an employee of the Health Board and was well-known in the area. Mareece Hannan, the almoner of the Coombe Hospital, was practically on their doorstep. Although the Coombe Hospital emphatically denied that she had ever worked there, some years later, I received a letter from a nun who assured me that Ms. Hannan had been an employee at the Coombe Hospital and was reconfirmed by Ms. Hannan's husband when I tracked him down about ten years later. She had passed away then, so he could not give me further information. I guess, in all respects, I was twenty years too late.

When I found out about my 'adoption', I also discovered that unbeknown to me, I belonged to a secret club of adoptees who would never be any the wiser. Initially, I thought I was alone in this experience as I had never heard a whisper about illegal adoptions in Ireland. Still, I soon discovered it was a very common, lucrative, and well-hidden practice. There were, in fact, thousands of us. The Irish State knew I was illegally registered, which they decided to keep secret. As described earlier, there was a written report about me until my sixteenth birthday.

I understand now that both my sisters had tried to persuade Kathleen to tell me that I had been 'adopted' Had I been informed, I could have tracked down the people involved, as many of them were still alive in the 1980s. In hindsight, I now realize that the truth would have come out if the social workers had rocked the boat. The illegal adoption/trafficking practice would have unfolded, and the professionals involved sent to prison. There was too much at stake financially for it to come into the public domain, and too many stood to gain financially from the deals.

Chapter 3
Endings and Beginnings
Goodbye, My Beloved Dad

My life changed forever on Monday, 25 January 1971. Kathleen was in England with Margaret, who had recently given birth to her first child, and Bernie and I had spent an enjoyable weekend with James. Little did we know it would be the last we would have together. I have a lasting memory of James that weekend, sitting at our dining table, pen in one hand, cigarette in the other, and laughing through the wisps of smoke that hung over him like a cloud waiting to unleash a thunderstorm. He was doing what he loved best: writing poetry.

When he got up on Monday morning, James complained of pains in his left arm that I shrugged off as merely cramping. (I was only fifteen and understandably unfamiliar with the symptoms of a heart attack). Our day started as normal, with me heading off to school and James traveling into the city, and I will never forget his smiling face looking at me through the bus window as I waved him goodbye—forever. When I was summoned out of class to say that I was needed urgently at home, I knew something horrible had happened to James. I remember sitting on the bus going home, trying to read a book but not taking in a single word. When I got home, my worst fears were realised. James had passed away. It was incomprehensible that this could happen to someone only fifty-two years old with no history of illness, a man who was so full of life and lived for his family.

The light in our home had been extinguished, in an instant. It was so incomprehensible that this had happened to us. At once, our once lively household felt like a morgue with grief hanging in the air. The memories of our home life are so sharp that it still hurts—

James coming in for tea full of joy, his eyes lighting up while relating a funny story to us as we sat around the table. Not one night went by where we weren't in heaps of laughter, with the sound echoing around our home. It wasn't just our family who felt the impact of James' death. He was a unique man who touched many people's lives in Dublin, and I remember well the outpouring of grief. But as happened at that time, no one ever spoke about their feelings.

I understand what people mean when they refer to someone dying of a broken heart. The pain I felt was intense. It felt like a giant hole had been hammered into my chest, like someone had taken a knife and cut a piece out of my heart. It hurt to breathe. My heart was broken. I hope I never have to experience such pain again. I know I will never get over the sense of loss, but I have become used to it. I thank God for our happy memories nearly fifty years later.

Despite Kathleen's negative feelings about me and the emotional problems she may have had, James and Kathleen had a wonderful relationship. James adored her, and his constant compliments to her were genuine, even though they amused Bernie and me. Kathleen stood by him through thick and thin, even when he was let go from jobs (often because he expressed his opinions at perceived injustice), and they had three mouths to feed. One of the happiest memories I have is of times when Bernie and I were in bed, and we would hear the hum of their voice's downstairs, talking and laughing until the early hours of the morning. It was a very comforting sound that drifted up to our bedroom.

My Beloved Dad James

Leaving Ireland

Life in our home in Rathfarnham changed forever on that day in January 1971. Readjustment to life without our beloved Dad was extremely difficult for Bernie and me. It was only in recent years, through the conversations, that we had both been separately grieving without knowing how to reach out to each other. He was the glue that kept our family together, and even now, over 50yrs later, we still cry over what happened. I guess death ends a life, not necessarily a relationship, and he will live in our hearts forever.

I was only fifteen, and Bernie, at thirteen, was even younger. We were still children who needed love and nurturing but were virtually ignored. Margaret was living in England, so Bernie and I did what we could for Kathleen and, in many ways, became adults. We ran the house, took Kathleen to the hairdresser, and went out for entertainment. But no matter how much we did for her, it never seemed enough. Would it have been any different had we been Kathleen's biological children? We will never know.

When I was nineteen, I knew I needed to find a way out of my labyrinth of grief and decided to go to England. To my surprise, Bernie broke down in tears the day I left, but I understood the separation would be difficult for her. We had been very close over the years, and she was now going to be alone in a house with a very gloomy atmosphere. But I had to think of myself, and on 24 April 1973, I set off on my adventure with my dear friend, Olive Kelly. I settled in Bournemouth, which is considered the riviera of the south of England with its beautiful beaches. Its temperate climate sharply contrasts with the rest of the UK and certainly Ireland! Not surprisingly, holiday-makers flock to the town in summer, creating a festive, happy atmosphere.

I felt I had been given a new lease of life and readily took to the lifestyle. I finally felt happy and began to forget the last four years of unpleasant, sad times. However, I didn't abandon my roots and kept in touch with my family, regularly sending money to Kathleen. In Bournemouth, I met and married my husband and had two beautiful children, Tara, and Ryan. My love for Tara when I first held her was indescribable. She felt wholly a part of me. A hole I hadn't known was part of my life was filled. My husband was from Brunei, and we moved to that country, living there for five years. However, we found the cultural differences too great, and our marriage did not last but I have always been grateful that he did remain in our children's lives and has been a good father.

The End of the Relationship

This is not a book about my relationship with Kathleen. However, undergirding my deeply rooted outrage at the illegal adoptions and the pain I have experienced is the rejection I experienced from Kathleen—my 'mother.' While I had felt the lack of a bond with Kathleen as I was growing up and sensed her coldness, I later experienced complete rejection on the few occasions I asked for help.

When my marriage broke up, I wanted to return to Ireland, the country I called home. Yearning to return to my roots and the culture that was part of my identity, I asked Kathleen whether my children and I could stay with her for a short time until I found my feet. Knowing my father would have welcomed us with open arms, I was dismayed when she came up with various excuses and eventually refused my request, to which I was shattered. Reluctantly, I returned to Bournemouth, where friends helped and supported me during that sad period of my life. I felt that my heritage had been stolen. (At this stage, I could not know that this was not the first time my heritage had

32

been stolen.) I never stopped asking, 'Why?' Why did she treat me as she did? Why did she not support me, her child? Why could she not help her child in times of trouble? I just could not fathom it.

The next time I faced Kathleen's complete rejection was when she lived in Inchicore. When I was thirty, I decided to try to restore our non-existent relationship, and with six-year-old Tara and two-year-old Ryan, I set off by bus from Rathfarnham to visit Kathleen. Never in my wildest dreams could I have anticipated how my life was to change that day. Waiting for buses and struggling with a buggy in the pouring rain was not a great way to spend Easter Monday, but I wanted my children to meet their grandmother. As we got off the bus, the heavens opened, and we were all drenched when we arrived at Kathleen's house. When I suggested that we could not go back in that weather and it would be better to stay for the night, Kathleen's demeanour changed, and I knew we would not be staying the night.

I thought my heart would break with the hurt and sense of rejection I was experiencing. That was when I decided to cut Kathleen out of my life. I would no longer tolerate ill-treatment towards myself and my children like we were strangers off the street. Our relationship finally ended on that Easter Monday in 1983, and I did not speak to Kathleen for the next eighteen years. Until the day I found out that she was not my mother.

James and Kathleen: Responsibility of Care

In Inchicore, my mother was highly regarded by her neighbours, who considered her a lovely, quiet woman with a strong moral code in line with her Catholic faith. She was held in high esteem; however, now and then, the veneer slipped. Bernie later gave me an example of this. Kathleen was asked by a neighbour, who was taking a collection for unmarried mothers, for a donation. The neighbour was taken aback when Kathleen said, *"They can rot in hell, as far as I am concerned"*.

"I think you had forgotten that I was an unmarried mother before I married, and so was your daughter. Or had you forgotten?" Kathleen tried to compose herself, but the damage had been done. She had unwittingly exposed her true feelings. The neighbour who previously held Kathleen in high esteem never spoke to her again.

When Bernie told me this story, I could not comprehend how she, as a fostered child, did not find Kathleen's attitude offensive. After all, her mother must have been unmarried which was confirmed at a later stage when Bernie finally met her. Just like my own mother, she had no choice but to surrender her baby, due to the attitude of the time in Ireland.

At that stage, I still had no idea that I was in the same category as Bernie. But my mother's comment sorely wounded my soul, and now the phrase *Children of a lesser God* springs to mind. In hindsight, perhaps Kathleen could never bond with me because, in her mind, I was the product of a sinful woman. To her, I was nothing. Sadly, many people in Ireland held (and probably still do) such archaic and harsh attitudes. Nevertheless, compassion and the responsibility to care for children and the vulnerable transcends any social conventions or mindsets.

Unlike Kathleen, James showed this compassion and responsibility of care. It was to James that people in Rathfarnham would come if their daughters became pregnant. He was completely non-judgemental and would do what he could to help the family with his many connections. On one occasion, James heard of an unmarried woman with a six-month-old baby in his hometown. Feeling shame and embarrassment, which was still very much part of the fabric of society in 1949, the young woman had not left her house nor had a visitor since the birth of her baby. My dad marched to the house and insisted on taking the baby out. He walked up and down the road with the baby happily gurgling in its pram. I can just imagine the talk in the town and the curtains twitching, but he didn't care. That child lived a happy life, being well brought up and loved. If there had been more people like my dad, Ireland would have been a better place, and there would not be thousands of bereft mothers who have spent a lifetime separated from their babies, nor children robbed of their culture, identity, and a mother's love.

PART 2: THE SEARCH

We must embrace pain and burn it as fuel for our journey.

Kenji Miyazawa – Japanese Novelist

Chapter 4
The Search for My Identity
Finding My File

At Bernie's insistence, I started my search to find out who I was. Earlier, encouraged by me, Bernie had looked for and found her natural mother. According to Bernie's birth certificate, her mother had an unusual name; by sheer coincidence, a friend of Bernie's worked with a woman in Dublin who had been best friends with her mother when they were young. It was a major shock for Bernie, but no one in Bernie's mother's family was aware that her mother had had a baby, so Bernie refrained from pushing it. I think she was just glad that she had found her mother. I have often wondered whether Bernie was fostered rather than being put up for adoption because her mother had hoped to come back for her but, due to lack of support, had not been able to do so. Her mother has shared her story with the thousands of women who wanted to keep their babies but did not have any support.

Bernie was convinced the Health Board would have information about me, so I applied for my records under the Freedom of Information Act. At first, I was told there were no records, but six months later, a large brown envelope landed on my doorstep out of the blue. Inside was a file and a letter from the Health Board stating that they had found a file in the archives and apologizing for the delay. Stunned, I sat and read the catalogue of events that had shaped my life—details about me at school, going to work, and what I looked like. It was a strange and unsettling experience. As stated earlier, I felt I had died and was reading my life story. I can't put it into words, but it was like I was reading about someone else, and it felt like my whole life was a lie.

I remember the social worker's monthly visits. At the time, I was told that she was visiting Bernie, who I knew had been fostered. I was told I needed to stay in the room so that Bernie didn't feel odd. I accepted this explanation. I can't remember being asked any questions, and now I presume the social worker just wanted to see that we were being looked after and still breathing. But Kathleen was petrified every time they appeared at the door. Although the Health Board never helped my parents financially, the social workers seemed to enjoy bullying Kathleen and constantly reminded her that her actions were illegal. Looking back from an adult perspective, I find it interesting that the social workers did not report Kathleen and just bullied her. Perhaps it was that they enjoyed using and abusing the power they had. She did not deserve that. James and Kathleen were good people and had 'adopted' me with the best motives.

It is also interesting that although the HSE kept a file on me and checked up on me regularly, it has never accepted responsibility for what happened to me, apportioning blame instead to James and Kathleen. When I sought legal advice, the solicitor's findings were:

> *It has been suggested by a legal representative that if the HSE hadn't allowed Ms. Tinggal to remain with her adoptive parents, she would have no doubt been placed in a home. It appears that the solution that the Health Board found to overcome the difficulty was to treat the arrangement as a foster placement (with no payment), which explains the frequency of the inspectors' visits to Ms. Tinggal's childhood home. The solution was not ideal, but a court would have some sympathy with the position that the Health Board found itself in.*

Seeking Legal Advice

No sympathy for my position, though.

The only clue to my identity was an index card I received twelve months later with the name of Margaret O'Grady (which I now know was not my name) and the words, 'Foster mother, Kathleen Hiney'. Neither the Health Board nor my adoptive family knew where the name came from. Given that the date of birth was the same as my own, I surmised (wrongly) that this must be my real name, and for the next fifteen years, I went on a wild goose chase, looking for any O' Grady's I thought may be related to me.

It was common practice for fictitious names to be given to babies and mothers all those decades ago. While the practice was no doubt to ensure anonymity, it made it almost heartbreakingly impossible decades later for either child or mother to search successfully for the other. I would have done anything at this stage to discover my real identity.

Meetings with Ministers

I was now on a mission to find my mother. I hoped she had been a very young woman when she gave birth to me, and there was still time for me to find her. (At the time, I did not know that she had been thirty-one when she had me.) Hope drove me, and I was determined to leave no stone unturned in my search for my birth mother. Things were changing in Ireland. Various advocacy groups were campaigning for changes to adoption legislation, and more and more people were approaching the media to search for their families. The secrets of the 1950s, which had been buried for decades, were starting to emerge.

I was on a mission to discover who I was and to find my birth mother. But now I was also on a mission to uncover how James and Kathleen had been allowed to illegally 'adopt' me with the authorities' knowledge. I set up a website *Adopted Illegally Ireland* and organised a peaceful demonstration outside the Bank of Ireland in Dame St, Dublin on 6th October 2011 with my colleague Maria Dumbell. Ms Dumbell found out she was 'adopted' when she applied for a passport. She discovered her birth was never registered and was only issued with an Irish passport after threatening a human rights lawsuit in Europe. She also has a document which shows the midwife who delivered her was state registered along with her foster mother. "The attitude of the Irish Government when I asked them for information was *'Well, things were done illegally then and we don't know who you are',"* she said.

Various members of the adoption community travelled from all over the country to support us. Sinn Féin TD Mary Lou McDonald joined the demonstration calling for legislation to be drafted. "I'm here to support adopted people in what I believe are very reasonable asks of the State concerning accessing their files and basic provisions available to people adopted that are living in other jurisdictions," she said. I had countless meetings with ministers in their capacities as Ministers for Children. The first of these was with Frances Fitzgerald, the first Minister of Children and Youth Affairs, who served from 2011 until 2014. Always, I was received politely but with blank stares. Despite my evidence and other people coming forward when they heard my story, I was met with stony silence. My story bored both Frances Fitzgerald and Minister Zappone. Frances Fitzgerald, at one point, asked a member of another adoptee advocate group, *'What exactly does that woman want?'* I was shocked that she could be so dismissive and show so little regard for those directly affected by such an egregious period in Irish history.

In 2016, I was at a meeting with Paul Redmond (Adoption Rights Now), Clodagh Malone (Beyond Adoption Ireland all Welcome), and Minister Zappone, the newly appointed Minister for Children. Also at the meeting was Anne Biggs a Banished Baby who had come from the U.S.A to tell her story to the Commission of Investigation (Information about the Commission of Investigation and the Banished Babies is presented in a later chapter). Anne was one of over 2,000 babies exported to America in the 1950s and 60s to Catholic families, being Catholic of course was a pre-requisite The State colluded with the Church to facilitate the export of thousands of 'illegitimate' children. A black market in babies was born and conveniently concealed by politicians. A very dark period in Irish history.

Then it was my turn: I had a ten-minute slot to tell my story, but mid-way through my account, Minister Zappone broke in and said, "Do we have to listen to Theresa all day?" This comment was greeted by stunned silence from all in the room. At this stage, I informed Minister Zappone that I had researched her background and thought she was a woman of justice up to that moment. *"Although you have to listen to the other cabinet members, sometimes you have to stand up for what is right and even, Minister, grow a pair of balls,"* I said directly to her. The sound of titters being stifled could be heard in the room, even from her own staff.

I had made my point. The comments made me conclude (rightly or wrongly) that the authorities have absolutely no interest in the illegal adoptees or empathy for their situation. They are happy to continue facilitating the secrecy surrounding the practice. What was conveyed to me was the ministers' complete lack of empathy and interest in a woman who was just trying to establish her real identity. I found this not only distressing but also shocking. I would have thought it obvious what I was looking for—my identity, which had been stolen from me. It was, after all, my right.

Under the umbrella of CMABS (Coalition of Mother and Baby Homes Survivors), which involved groups such as Adopted Illegally Ireland, Adoption Rights Now, Mixed Race Irish, Bethany Homes, as well as individuals including Catherin Corless (historian) Terri Harrison and David Kinsella, we were granted a meeting with James

Reilly, the then Minister for Children and Youth Affairs. He seemed very empathetic and interested in our stories, and, for once, we felt that there was someone who was genuinely listening to us. Much to our disappointment, there was a cabinet reshuffle the day after our meeting, and he was appointed to serve elsewhere.

In hindsight, I realize the authorities had been aware of illegal adoptions/registrations for years but had done nothing. Now they were being confronted by me, an unknown adoptee living on the other side of the water who wanted answers. For them, dealing with someone who wanted answers had always been to keep quiet. *Deny everything. Keep quiet, and they will eventually go away* seemed to be their modus operandi.

I keep wondering why. Why did the Department of Children deliberately obstruct and constantly reject appeals for an investigation? Why did officials in the department never share files with successive ministers? Eventually, the government ordered a full investigation due to pressure from interested groups. Details of this are given in Part 6, Chapter 11 of this book.

I Continue Searching for My Mother

Despite the lack of interest from the ministers, this woman— Theresa Tinggal—was not going anywhere! I had no intention of ever giving up my search. I wrote passionate letters to every adoption society and former mother and baby home, pleading for information on my mother's whereabouts. I also contacted every newspaper in Ireland, with some prominent ones printing my story. I was interviewed on TV and radio and waited with bated breath, hoping my mother would read my articles, recognize me, and a reunion would happen. During that time, I had emails from people worldwide who thought they might be related to me. I jumped on planes following up leads in Ireland but to no avail.

To say that I was exhausted is an understatement, and I lived in a state of desperation for years. I was, however, amazed at how helpful and empathic some people were when they read my articles in the various newspapers, suggesting various avenues for me to approach. I always followed their suggestions. I was like a demented person who went to great lengths to seek answers. At one time, albeit with a rather cynical attitude, I resorted to reversion therapy, hoping that under hypnosis, I could return to my birth and perhaps my mother's name may come up. That is what I was looking for: a name. Alas, I got nothing positive from that session, but it was another possibility that was ticked off my list.

I had to try everything. I was so desperate that I decided to travel three hundred miles to Glasgow to see a supposedly excellent psychic who had been recommended to me. *Psychic to the Stars,* her internet profile states, and the fact that she helps the police to solve missing persons/murders convinced me that she would be able to help me. At last, I was going to get some answers. After waiting in eager anticipation for some months for my appointment, I arrived at the house just to be told that the psychic was not there. She had had to go away. My world collapsed once more, and I burst into tears. I was inconsolable. Months of hoping just evaporated. The housekeeper invited me in and made me a cup of tea, trying to calm me down. While I was sobbing, I told her my story.

Myself, Maria Dumbell and Paul Redmond (Adoption Rights Now) at a press conference with member of parliament Clare Daly

While I was in the psychic's living room, I noticed a lot of photos of her with celebrities. Celebrities probably would have paid a lot of money to see her. How true, I wonder, were her revelations? I could only see a prima donna who liked to mix with celebrities. I was annoyed that I hadn't been contacted and been able to cancel the long journey that I had made. Although I was assured, they had tried to call me, I doubted their excuse as I had been at home the whole time before traveling there. The psychic even had the cheek to email me to say that I needed special help, totalling lacking in empathy for my situation. Such is the desperation of anyone engaging in such searches. We are extremely vulnerable and need someone by our side to help us through the disappointments and people who let us down along the way.

I often wonder if my real mother ever read one of my desperate pleas and felt it necessary to disclose her secret to her 'daughter' in the unlikely event that I ever turned up. I think that she did.

45

Nurse Doody's Register

In 2011, I received an email from Nurse Doody's grandson. While clearing out St Jude's nursing home on Howth Road, he found a register in the attic dated from 1938 to 1968 with over 1,000 births registered.

Dear Theresa,

I found your story on the internet and got your email address from your posting on http://books.dreambook.com/kathymcmahon/mathairail.html.

My name is James Doody, and I am the grandson of the Nurse Doody of 84 Collins Ave, and I have obtained my grandmother's Register of Cases.

I have found an entry for you, but unfortunately, I don't think it will help you trace your birth mother.

I have attached photographs of the original register, but the important details that I have are as follows:

Name/Address of Patient: Mrs C Hiney, 518 Carnlough Rd, Cabra.

Age: 32

Date/Time of Child's Birth: 11.30 pm 9.6.54

Doctor: Dr Keane, Mount Merron.

Date of Midwife's last visit: 17/6/54

If you wish, I am happy to discuss the details with you, or if you want to view the records, I can meet you sometime in Dublin.

I wish you all the best in your search.

Regards, James Doody

No.	Date of expected Confinement	Name and Address of Patient	Age	No. of previous Labours and Miscarriages	Date and hour of Midwife's Arrival	Presentation	Date and hour of Child's Birth	Sex of Infant Born Living or Dead	Full time or Premature No. of Weeks	Name of Doctor, If called
181	11/6/54	Mrs. C. Finery 518 Cavenlough Rd Cabra	32	1	6 P.M. / 8 ... / 6 P.M / 8. 6. 54	◿ / 2. 0	11.30 PM / 9.6.54	F	F/T	Dr Keane Mount Merrion

CASES.

Name of Doctor, if called	Complications (if any) during or after Labour	Date of Midwife's last visit	Condition of Mother then [See Rules, Rule 16, p. 10]	Condition of Child then Section E, p. 10]
John Keane Joseph Kerrion	none	17/6/54	Good	G.
			Good.	G
				G

	Condition of Mother then [See Rules, Rule 16, p. 10]	Condition of Child then Section E, p. 10]	REMARKS
	Good	G.	—
	Good.	G.	—
	Good	Good	—

I was so excited! Perhaps this file would hold details of my mother and, at last, furnish proof of what had been going on. I met James Doody in Dublin, who kindly let me look at the register. It was a nondescript foolscap (A3) document, something that shopkeepers once would have used to record their orders. However, it was important for me. It held some of our birth details, although they were not entirely true. This record contained a thousand births, some illegal and some just ordinary births. Anyone can be recognised only by their date of birth and their adoptive name. I am one of the lucky ones that have a file. Without that, I would have nothing to confirm that I ever existed. My entry just said, 'Theresa Marion Hiney, Mother Kathleen Hiney: born Carnlough Road Cabra: delivered by Dr Keane'. This was all false. The doctor may not have even been present, and although the entry states that the midwife's (Nurse Doody) last visit was 17th June, after collecting me on 11th June, Kathleen never saw Nurse Doody again.

Understandably, James kept the original register but provided Tusla (Child and Family agency) with a copy. Clare Daly TD (member of parliament), who supported us greatly, asked to see the file and produced it in the Dáil (parliament) as evidence, but the government still did nothing. In the many cases of people asking for my help, the adoptive parents have been named as the natural parents. However, the Irish government seemed to believe that this was not enough to start an investigation into illegal adoptions, therefore, excluding illegal adoptions from the Commission of Investigation!

The disappointment in the voices of people searching for their identity when I give them the results is always heart-breaking. We all cling to hope every time something new emerges, but nothing is easy when you are illegally registered as someone else's child. Knowing that there is a file from a former nursing home signifies that there could be more, and these former homes need to be investigated for evidence for us!

Chapter 5
Finding My Family

DNA

After all my wild goose chases over the years, I decided that the only option open to me was to register on a DNA website. Several people had encouraged me to do this, so feeling that I had nothing to lose, I registered on one of the best-known DNA websites, Ancestry DNA, and discovered the joys of DNA tracing. An international survey of 1200 adoptees, conducted between October 2016 and April 2017, revealed that over fifty per cent had found a sibling or a parent through DNA tracing; of these, eight percent had found their parent or sibling waiting for them as soon as they opened their results.[4] Since then, the number of people in the DNA databases has increased from about eight million to about twelve million, so the 2017 figures are already outdated. The results are a hundred per cent accurate, as the DNA does not lie to you. The facts are there in black and white to make of them what you will.

To confirm what I had been told, I spoke to Dr Maurice Gleeson, who offered further information. He sent me the following information:

Most of us are fortunate enough to know who our parents are and if we have any brothers or sisters. But for many people, this information is simply unavailable, and they do not possess the basic information about their origins. Foundlings and abandoned babies usually have no documentation regarding their birth parents. Illegitimate children may know who their birth mother was but not their birth father. The same applies to donor-conceived children.

[4] M Gleeson. https://www.irishrootsmedia.com/blog/item/using-dna-to-trace-your-birth-family-by-dr.-maurice-gleeson/43

Adoptees may not be allowed access to their birth records, or such documentation may have been forged. For many, this leaves them with a sense of rootlessness, of not belonging, and leads to an overwhelming need to discover who were the people who gave them life and what were the circumstances of their coming into being.

It is pertinent never to lose sight of the fact that no matter how lost to him his natural parents may be, the adopted child carries stamped in every cell of his body genes derived from his fore bearers. The primitive stuff of which he is made and which he will pass on to future generations was determined finally at the time of his conception... The implications of this for the psychology of the adopted child are of utmost significance.
Florence Clothier, M.D.

facebook.com/isadoptiontrauma?

The lack of access to (or complete absence of) birth documentation is a huge obstacle to anyone of unknown parentage who is trying to trace their birth families. But the advent of commercial DTC (direct-to-consumer) DNA testing has largely circumvented this problem, and many people have been reconnected with their birth families through DNA testing. There are countless stories of such reunions in the press, television, and on YouTube. DNA has even solved 'historic' cases of unknown parentage relating to the parents or grandparents of people living today.

Several companies offer DTC DNA testing. For anyone interested in pursuing the DNA route, I recommend testing with Ancestry first and transferring a copy of your DNA data (for free) to My Heritage, Family Tree DNA, Living DNA, and Gedmatch. This is the most cost-effective approach. For added privacy, you can use initials instead of your full name or even a fake name – whichever you prefer. If you do not identify your birth family via these websites, you can test with 23andMe. The cost of these tests is less than $100 (and frequently less than $50 in the Christmas sales); thus, DNA testing will be very affordable for most people.

The process is quite simple. You buy the DNA test online, the DNA kit is posted to you, you swab your cheek or provide a saliva sample into a small plastic tube, you post it back to the company, and in about three to six weeks, you will receive an email informing you that your DNA results are back from the lab. You then sign into the account created for you on the company website, and you will be presented with a list of 'DNA matches'–that is, people with whom you share the exact segments of DNA, thus indicating that you have a common ancestor. The more DNA is shared, the closer the relationship.

The next step is to contact these matches (via the website or the email they have supplied) and figure out how you are related. You will find a close family member among your matches if you are very lucky. A 2016 survey of 1200 adoptees (mainly from the US) found that when they first received their DNA results, two percent found a birth parent among their matches, six percent found a half-sibling, five percent found an uncle or aunt, and nineteen percent found a first cousin. [1] Close matches usually result in a very quick search resolution, and you may be reunited with your birth family within days of receiving your results.

Since this 2016 survey, the size of the DNA databases has increased dramatically, reaching close to forty million people in 2020. And as the database size increases, finding family becomes easier and easier. However, for many people, their closest DNA matches may indicate a second or third-cousin relationship, and a little bit of hard work will be needed to figure out the connection. Second cousins have a set of great-grandparents in common and third cousins have a set of great-great-grandparents in common. So if you were born in 1950, your connection to a second cousin would be great-grandparents who might have been born in the 1860s (or thereabouts).

Similarly, your connection to a third cousin would be further back, possibly in the 1830s. This is where genealogical research comes into play, and it will be necessary to trace the family trees of your DNA matches to the 1800s (and possibly to the 1700s). If you are not a genealogist yourself, this can be a daunting task. But help is at hand. Various Facebook groups are staffed by volunteers who offer free help and assistance (e.g., DNA Detectives, Search Squad). Also, many experienced genealogists online can offer their assistance for free or for a professional fee.

Here is a summary of the process involved in finding the birth family by using more distant DNA matches (i.e., second, third, or more distant cousins):

1. Identify clusters of 'Shared Matches' (i.e., people among your matches who all match each other and are likely to share a common ancestor). If you are lucky, you will identify four distinct clusters for each grandparent.

2. Starting with the cluster with the closest matches, identify family trees for everyone in that cluster (for those matches who do not have family trees or who only have limited family trees, you will need to build the family tree yourself using available records and any information you can glean by contacting the match in question).

3. Find the common ancestor (or common ancestral couple) for each cluster and trace all their descendants (down to your birth parents' generation).

4. Define your own relative position in the resultant family tree for each cluster (by assessing the amount of DNA you share with others in the cluster, aided by tools such as the Shared cM Tool and the WATO tool on the DNA Painter website).

5. Identify where descendants of one cluster intersect with descendants of another cluster (e.g., Someone from cluster A marries someone from cluster D). This is likely to identify one set of grandparents. In this case, one of their children will be either your genetic father or your genetic mother.

This process is an example of genetic genealogy, where DNA and standard genealogical research are combined to solve genealogical questions, including identifying a birth family. This same genetic genealogy technique has applications beyond family-tree research and adoptee searches. It is being used successfully to identify unidentified human remains and perpetrators of violent crimes, the most famous case to date being that of the Golden State Killer in California. Such is the power of this genetic genealogy technique that the FBI has set up its own investigative genetic genealogy unit, and other countries are following suit.

I have been helping adoptees find their birth families for several years, and this book's author (Theresa Tinggal) was among the first of my clients in Ireland. At the time of writing, Irish adoption records remain closed and new legislation to address this is currently in limbo. Therefore, DNA testing is the only way forward for many Irish people searching for their birth families. Similarly, for Irish mothers who gave birth to children who were subsequently adopted, DNA may be the only way of finding their children. In 2019, one such mother was reunited with her child when a new person suddenly appeared among her DNA matches twelve months after she had taken the test. She had never been told whether she'd had a boy or a girl, so it was an inexpressible relief (after sixty years of not knowing) to learn that she had given birth to a son.

DNA can bring closure as it can help answer questions that have remained unanswered for a lifetime. DNA can restore a sense of identity and relieve a burden carried around for decades. It is no wonder that this kind of search is an emotional rollercoaster for all parties concerned. It is, therefore, essential to consider the following:

1. Anyone undertaking this kind of search should have a support network at hand and preferably undertake it with the assistance of a trained professional (social worker, counsellor, or otherwise).

2. Professional help is also particularly useful when juggling the competing rights of the searcher and the birth family and making judgment calls on all the possible sensitivities involved.

3. Many people undertaking these searches also need help crafting carefully worded correspondence with potential birth family members. You may only have one chance to get it right.

4. It is also important to manage the expectations of both the person searching and the members of the birth family. Television programs (like Long Lost Family) would have us believe that every search has an easily achieved happy ending. This is not the case. Every search comes with its twists and turns. It is not unusual to have a shocking piece of information revealed that leaves the searcher reeling. It is wise to expect the totally unexpected.

5. It takes time to digest new information as it emerges, to work through emotional revelations, and to come to terms with a new reality and a different outcome from the one initially expected.

6. And the work does not stop there. Building a relationship with your family is a lifelong process, whether you knew them from birth or met them in adulthood. DNA has opened new doors for foundlings, adoptees, donor-conceived people, and all people of unknown parentage. But it takes a lot of work to arrive at a conclusion and to accept the results.

I wish everyone embarking on this journey all the best wishes in the world. Take your time, be cautious, be conservative, and put yourself in the other person's shoes. But above all, be kind to yourself and others.[5]

After so many knocks, at long last, I began to feel positive. I realized I was unlikely to get results straight away, but I knew I was on the right road and was taking control of my life. As Dr Gleeson noted, tracing your family this way can be an emotional rollercoaster for everyone concerned and a journey not to be undertaken lightly. Having a support network, getting professional help, preparing what you will say to your new-found family, and dealing with upsets and surprises—these journey elements need to be considered before going down the DNA route. The reconnection with a parent or sibling is

---

[5] Maurice Gleeson Education Ambassador ISOGG (International Society of Genetic Genealogy) November 2020

immediate for the eight percent of adoptees whose first search gives results.

The Breakthrough

My DNA search took many twists and turns. After about a year, I discovered a first cousin match in America through that cousin's sister, Breda (not her real name), who had started a family tree. Breda and my cousin had both been 'adopted' from Ireland along with their two 'brothers'. Each of the children had been adopted separately from Ireland, and it was the first time they heard the term 'Banished Babies'. When told about the practice, Breda was shocked and was adamant that her parents would not have known the truth. I presume those involved made sure that the adoptive parents did not know all the facts and were probably told that the mother had died or had willingly given her baby up for adoption. Unknown to Breda's adoptive parents and all the others who freely gave 'donations' to the Church, many of the birth mothers had been given no choice.

While the cousin I found in America was not interested in helping with my search, the trail did lead to Tipperary, and I discovered who her mother was. Her mother's niece took a DNA test to see if there was a match with mine, but it transpired that the relationship between us was on the father's side.

I informed my cousin that I had found her mother who was very ill in the local hospice, but she did not pursue the connection. She had only submitted the Ancestry DNA for fun and to assemble a family tree. She informed me that she had a very happy life, had no negative feelings about being adopted, and did not feel the need to seek her biological parents. I respected her decision to have no further contact with me. Nevertheless, I now could add another piece to the puzzle.

58

The emotional impact of continuous searching and being disappointed time and time again took its toll on me. Feeling I was back to where I had started, I needed to take a step back. I stopped my search for approximately two years.

Then a DNA match was discovered in New Zealand, leading to Tipperary, but there was no information about to whom I was matched, so it was with great trepidation that I returned to Ireland. I was hoping it would be my mother, but any breakthrough would have been welcome. I was very anxious that I would again be rebuffed, but this time the family was more than happy to help me from the moment I met them. Meeting Helen (not her real name), who turned out to be my first cousin, was a joyful experience. After showing her my DNA results and pointing out my grandparents, she surprisedly said, 'But they are also my grandparents! I need to help you. What do you want me to do?'

'If you are willing to have a further DNA test to confirm things, that would be great, I replied, and there and then, it was decided. I was elated at her thoughtful response and was invited to meet her brother the next morning. Her sister also turned up, so I was in the company of three cousins I had never met before. It felt so surreal, yet so natural. Helen had previously read accounts of my story online, but the others were all a bit shell-shocked as we went over and over my story during the next couple of hours. Because we were unsure whether we were siblings or cousins, another DNA test was vital to establish our relationship. It seemed most likely that Helen and I had the same father, which would make us siblings, or that her aunt (her father's sister) was my mother. The latter was the case: her aunt was my mother. I was very sad that my mother had passed away eight years before.

Having identified my mother, we realized that there was a strong possibility that I may have a sibling. This turned out to be correct. What I thought then was a sister, called Brigid (not her real name). I was very excited by the news, but when Brigid was phoned with the news, her reaction was very different from the warm welcome I had had from my cousins. She was quite frosty, and her only question was, *'What is her name?'* Not, *'What does she look like?'* or *'Why does she think she is related to us?'* This was followed by stony silence at the end of the phone.

Sean, (not his real name) who was making the call, appeared slightly embarrassed and said that Brigid would speak to him later. She did indeed speak to him—her main concern was how accurate DNA was. Sean, who works with cattle, was more than able to highlight how it all worked and could tell her that the results were definite. *"Do you think Theresa will leave it now that she has found her family?"* she asked my cousins. *What a strange question*, I thought. I had just turned up and wanted to get to know all of them. No! Certainly, this woman was going nowhere. I had been so excited at the thought of having a sibling I naively thought that she would feel the same and was disappointed when she showed no interest in meeting me. She kept stressing that no one was to know about this, but Theresa, who had fought for 15 years to get information about her mother, was not going to be swept under any carpet—she was looking for her identity!

I managed to get Brigid to agree to see me. I was so eager to hear about my mother. What did she look like? Did she have green eyes like mine? What was her personality? Nearly everyone has eyes that are brown, blue, green, or somewhere in between. Grey or hazel eyes are less common. I was shocked yet amused that Brigid didn't know the colour of my mother's eyes and couldn't (or perhaps wouldn't) tell me anything about my mother's young life. When I eventually, with much coercion, managed to see a photo of my mother, I was struck by my resemblance to her; yes, she had green eyes!

However, what surprised and disconcerted me was that Brigid was nothing like my mother or me, either physically or in manner. Unlike my cousins, I saw no kindness in her and could not believe we were related! But were we related? Interestingly, my cousins had been eager to take a DNA test proving that Helen was my first cousin, but Brigid steadfastly refused a test. It seemed beyond belief that this woman, who had been brought up as the daughter of Alice Monica, would not want to verify a stranger's claims to be her biological sister. Hmmm.

I have pondered what motivated Brigid to keep me out of her life. The clearest explanation for me was that she was still a victim of the culture that regarded illegitimacy as a 'sin'. She did not want her reputation tainted by an unexplained half-sister who had suddenly come into her life. Another explanation could be a fear that she would have to share her inheritance (although this was the last thing on my mind). As explained earlier, land has always held a special place in the national psyche of the Irish people. Historically, this comes from the times of famine when people were evicted from their land. The trauma is inscribed in our DNA and is culturally transmitted.

Brigid's comment that her life '…was fine until you came along' also applied to me. My life was also fine until that fateful day when I discovered I was not who I thought I was. Ultimately, I feel that Brigid and I are both the losers: our differences in how we react to our circumstances have been too great to overcome.

Family Links

I decided to pursue another DNA match and knocked on the door of the contact I had found. It turned out that this was my uncle, my father's brother, although I didn't know of the connection at the time. After I had disclosed why I was there and had briefly told my story, I was invited in, and tea was made. Now in their eighties, Marion and John didn't really get the concept of DNA, but their attitude was, '*Sure. If we're related, that's grand*'. What beautiful non-judgemental, accepting sentiments! Although there was a match with the cousin who had popped up in America, I wanted to be sure that this lovely man sitting opposite me, who just wanted to welcome me into the family, was a blood relative. Looking into his face and seeing family photos scattered around the living room, I realized I was not unlike them. I thought it might be that I wanted to look like and connect with someone I could relate to, so while I tried to shrug the feeling off, I was really hoping! Uncle John had my mannerisms, nose, and sense of humour, and I kept staring intently at him. Could I dare believe we were related?

I mentioned that I hoped he would agree to take a DNA test, but I quickly realized that he didn't understand what I was asking. He had told me about his sons and daughter, so I approached one of them instead. I didn't hold out much hope as I, a stranger, would be asking them to do something quite personal. I needn't have worried as Michael agreed straight away. I considered myself the luckiest woman in those few days. Meeting two beautiful families who were my flesh and blood and kind and welcoming were priceless. Michael did take the test to confirm the relationship, and when he showed up as a first cousin, I felt as if I had won the lottery! Bingo. I had found the other half of my family.

Michael invited me to his home for Sunday dinner on my next visit. The whole family was there: his mother, father (my uncle, whom I had met first), his lovely wife, and their two sons. His sister and her husband came up from Dublin, and boxes of old family photos were brought down. There was much hilarity that afternoon as we looked at the resemblances and talked about the personalities of people staring out at me, now long dead, like my family. It was decided unanimously that I resembled Granny, a small, slight woman who, I was told, had a lot of attitudes. Yes, I could identify with that description, alright. They were so welcoming; they were lovely people, and it was more than I had ever dreamed of.

Now that I had found my family—people who looked like me with mannerisms mirroring mine—I felt complete and, at last, had a sense of identity. Most people take genetic links for granted; I take after my grandmother's or *my mother's eyes* had never been there for me. Now, I love hearing stories about my mother and seeing her photos. I have her mouth and green eyes, and on my father's side, *you have the attitude of Granny*. My soul at last felt a sense of peace.

Interestingly, in 2019 a woman in Clogheen, Co Tipperary, contacted me through private messaging on Facebook. She had read an article about me in the *Tipperary Star* (a local newspaper) about my poignant visit to my mother's grave on my 65th birthday—sixty-five years after my mother had been forced to relinquish me and the tenth anniversary of her death. This woman was very excited and was keen to speak to me on the phone, and privately messaged me on Facebook:

Hi, you don't know me, but I am a niece of Mona, well, her husband's niece actually. I only saw your notice in the Nationalist this morning. It explains a lot about Mona, the lady I knew. I would love to meet you, but I will understand if you prefer not to.

My reply was sent on 29 August 2019

Oh, I would love to hear so much about my mam. Can I phone you later on messenger?

Her reply

You can certainly call me. I'm minding 6 children today and working in the local golf club at 5.30 tomorrow morning after 9.30 or anytime Saturday up to 2 pm. I would love to talk today, but I would be afraid it wouldn't happen with the kids.

Thank you for replying.

After countless calls and messages to her were left unanswered, I knew that Brigid had probably intervened and warned her to have nothing to do with me. I wonder what she was afraid of. I have a right to information about my mother, but no one thinks so, whether it be the ordinary man in the street or the government! How sad that Brigid never even tried to get to know me. She has no other brothers or sisters or, indeed, children. I think my mother would turn in her grave at her behaviour. I do not doubt that she knew about me. She was indeed shocked when I turned up, but I am guessing it was because I did turn up and not because my mother had a baby out of wedlock. However, I suspect there are other reasons!

The message stating, 'It explains a lot about Mona, the lady I knew,' confirms that my mother's behaviour toward outsiders was not normal. She had a hidden side, perhaps a sad side, a secret that she could not tell. My heart breaks for her having to live a lie and all through no fault of her own but because of the Church and society. I constantly worried about what happened to my mother, and the thought of her being cruelly treated made my heart sad. Perhaps she had seen first-hand what had happened to girls who got pregnant and decided to take a different route. In her case, I certainly think that she did the right thing.

Chapter 6
Filming of Adoption Stories

In 2015, I was asked to appear on the show, *Adoption Stories.*

This was the same time I had decided to register on a DNA tracing website, and I had not yet found any family members.

When I first met Sharon Lawless, the producer, in the lounge at Heathrow airport, I knew she was a woman with a huge amount of empathy for people who had experienced what I had. Based on the popular TV3 series, the show illustrates what happened to mothers and adoptees and offers a fascinating window into the extraordinary experience of natural parents, adopted children, and their adoptive families. On the show, people share their experiences and discuss the impact adoption has had on their lives. Since 1952, nearly 45,000 babies have been legally adopted in Ireland, and it has been estimated that a similar number of illegal adoptions have taken place simultaneously (from *Adoption Stories* by Sharon Lawless). I hoped and prayed that someone somewhere would watch the show and recognize my story or that I might bear a striking resemblance to a family member. I waited with bated breath, but once again, nothing materialized.

Another two years had passed when Sharon Lawless again approached me. This time it was for a follow-up show: *Adoption Stories: What Happened Next?* I can't thank Sharon and her research staff enough for what must have been hundreds of hours they put into uncovering this jigsaw-puzzle life of mine. I had started a degree with the Open University, which had taken priority, so I was eternally grateful to be able to hand over the information and DNA history that kept popping up. Trying to negotiate your way through all the data can feel like a minefield. Still, thankfully there are lots of Facebook groups, such as DNA Detectives, DNA Newbies, Irish Adoption Database and DNA MatchFinder who are more than willing to help you navigate this beautiful genetic map.

It's a Long Way to Tipperary

By sheer coincidence, the filming for *Adoption Stories: What happened next?* Coincided with the discovery of my family in Tipperary. I had just returned from a visit to Australia and immediately took another flight to Ireland to appear in the documentary. We decided to film some of the beauty spots in and around Cahir and Clogheen, Co Tipperary, finishing off at the grave of the woman I had been searching for, years: my mother. I was unfortunate that my long search had ended in a graveyard, but I took comfort from the fact that I had found my family beyond my expectations. Although I would have kept searching forever, I had, at times, become despondent. But every time I hit a brick wall, something deep inside me told me never to give up. It was almost as though my mother was pushing me on.

I nestled at the foot of the Galtee mountains in St John the Baptist church, its only company the headstones of the deceased in the graveyard, telling the brief life stories of the villagers. The headstones connect related families; once part of this community, they are now all gone. In the church are examples of the work of the famous artist Harry Clarke in the form of stained-glass depicting Salome presenting the head of John the Baptist to Herod and another showing Lourdes's Apparition. There my mother was, with other family members, in a country graveyard framed by the beautiful mountains in the distance. My eyes rested on her name for what seemed like an eternity. I did not want to leave her. I felt that my heart was hearing her voice as if she were right there with me and her smile was one of happiness. It had taken sixty-four years, but at last, we were together. My arduous journey had come to an end. As I sat there in this place of peace and solace, I imagined my mother praying in this church Sunday after Sunday, year after year. I hoped that she had prayed for me.

That day was a beautiful spring day. With the sun shining, it was a perfect ending to the filming of *Adoption Stories. What happens next?* At first, the priest was open to our request to film inside the church, and he was very sympathetic to my story. We spent several hours filming both inside the church and in the graveyard. Eventually, we reluctantly left and headed to Dublin for me to catch my flight back to England. Sitting on the plane and staring into space, I had to pinch myself. Had this really happened? I had found my family after all my years of searching! Through sheer perseverance and DNA tracing, I eventually found who I was after sixty-four years. The missing pieces had fallen into place, and at last my heart felt at peace.

Finding my mother's grave

Adoption Stories: Version Two

A couple of weeks after I had arrived back from Australia had been a whirlwind of emotions, but now that the filming for *Adoption Stories* was over, I started to settle back into my everyday life. It was a shock, therefore, when Sharon Lawless informed me that the priest had changed his mind and had withdrawn his permission for us to use the film we had taken inside the church and the graveyard at my own mother's grave! I immediately phoned the priest to ask for his reasons and was told that he had to protect his parishioners. He said he didn't want to discuss the matter further but that if he could help, he would. He didn't need to mention names, but I knew he was referring to Brigid. Before putting the phone down, my retort was, *'You can, but you won't.'*

My God! Here we were, sixty-four years after my mother had given birth to me, and the clergy was still calling the shots. Further, Brigid's husband had approached a solicitor to prevent us from using the film. Interestingly, he did not go to his local solicitor in Tipperary but to one in a neighbouring county. He couldn't risk people knowing that an illegitimate daughter of his wife's mother had turned up. *Sure, what would people think, or was there another reason, I wonder?* The letter's tone was very dismissive, stating that 'Ms Tinggal has no documentary proof or evidence to support Ms Tinggal's contention that the said Mrs (name not given to protect her identity) may be her mother.' I did have documentary proof, but Brigid was not interested in seeing it, nor was she interested in making my acquaintance, as noted in the solicitor's letter:

> *Our client would like to wish Teresa Tinggal every success in her search for her natural mother, and if Teresa Tinggal is a relation of our client, then in that event, our*

client will be more than happy to meet with Ms Tinggal and to make acquaintance with her.

As mentioned earlier, we did meet up, but only at my insistence, and Brigid remained cold and unfriendly throughout the meeting. She refused to meet me again in 2019 when I was in Tipperary.

Sharon asked me if I would return to Ireland to refilm the shots another way. I was on that plane and off to Tipperary again without hesitation. It is a long way, alright! There is surely a way where there is a will, and I had not come so far in my search for the end of it to be spoiled by small-minded people. A graveyard is a public place, so I had every right to be there. We took the same shots at my mother's grave with the camera team using a long lens from outside the graveyard.

As we were rounding everything up, a man approached me and asked whether I was Theresa, introducing himself as Brigid's husband. He proceeded to tell me that he was not happy with the filming in the graveyard. I reminded him that it was my mother's grave and that the story of my illegal 'adoption' was being filmed as a documentary. It would bring hope to people who, like me, were going through or had gone through life without legal papers, never knowing who they were. I told him my story of how I had found out about being adopted and my subsequent search for the truth. I assured him that we would be as discreet as possible and did not intend to hurt anyone. We just wanted to tell the truth. The camera team confirmed what I had said. The camera crew and I very quickly realized that this little man was not listening and was really not interested in what I had to say.

Despite attempts by Brigid and her husband to prevent the filming, the documentary was completed and aired on Irish TV3, shortly after I had discovered my family. It was too much to take in, and I was emotionally and mentally exhausted when I arrived back in the UK. I still had to pinch myself. Had this finally happened? All my years of searching had come to fruition.

My Health Suffers

Alas, the psychological stress I had unknowingly been under caught up with me. I say 'unknowingly' because I had kept going like the proverbial dog with a bone, looking for answers without thinking of the effect on my health. As well my search for answers, I read for a degree at the Open University, graduating in 2018. But then things started to catch up with me. In 2019 I started to feel unbelievably tired. In fact, that really is an understatement. Once I returned home from work, I would sleep for at least four hours, basically going from work to bed and then from bed to work.

Having always been a fit, healthy woman, I was really worried at this turn of events. My sister told me it was to be expected, saying, *"Well, that's what happens when you start getting old"*! I had just turned sixty-five when things started to go wrong, so I reluctantly began to agree with her. I felt that I was falling apart and was both physically and mentally drained. I developed two tooth abscesses, one after the other, which required extensive dental work, and to cap it all, I developed shingles on my head! My doctor sent me for blood tests and discovered that I had a low-functioning thyroid. Thankfully this is treatable, and my energy has returned.

PART 3: ADOPTION EXPERIENCES

Chapter 7
Personal Experiences

As I mentioned earlier, I discovered I was part of a whole community of people in the same situation. Mothers forced to give up their babies are told they should forget about their babies, move on with their lives, and have more children and that their babies will never miss them. People presume that a person who has been adopted when just a few days old will accept their adopted family as their own and never be concerned about from where they came. But there is story after story debunking this thinking. Mothers tell how they never gave up looking for their children, and children tell stories of how they spent years looking for their mothers and have never felt part of the family. Always something missing. My own story bears testament to this. In this chapter, I present the stories of people who describe their experiences.

Kevin Battle

Kevin Battle, a retired police officer in Portland, Maine, U.S.A., was one of the thousands of Banished Babies. As reported in *The Irish Times* on 9 September 2021, he had been 'adopted' from the Sean Ross Abbey mother and baby home, Co Tipperary. He only found out about his Irish family when he was given a DNA kit as a present by chance and began searching for his birth mother. He found out that his mother had been forced to give him up for adoption, and a family in the U.S.A. had paid a thousand dollars.

It took four decades to discover his mother's identity. Adoption records from fifty or sixty years ago were often sealed and inaccessible, or they were inaccurate. Kevin reports that he was brushed off when he turned up at the mother and baby's home. At one stage, he was told by a nun that his mother had died, which was not valid at the time. However, through DNA he eventually found the Irish family he never knew he had. Discovering that his mother had died in 2009 but to his delight, he was told that she had been looking for him. He said, *"They were looking for me. They knew about me. I always wanted to hear that from somebody."* He found a cousin and discovered that he had half-siblings—two brothers and three sisters—who live in Wales and whom he has visited.

"I always had the feeling of not fitting in, but when I went to Wales, and we went to this place to eat, looking around at my brothers, I felt welcome. And I felt like I belonged." he said.

Tressa Reeves[6]

When Tressa Reeves gave birth to a son, she wanted to keep him, but her mother forbade it. Left alone with him for just one night, she secretly baptized him, calling him André, an unusual name. She did this deliberately as she felt it would be easier for her to find him later on, and in the 1970s, she decided to track him down.

When Tressa approached the St Patrick's Guild adoption society, a nun told her that there was no file and that she must have imagined giving birth to a baby. (As if any woman could imagine being pregnant for nine months and then the pain of childbirth!) Despite hitting a brick wall with the nuns in St Patrick's Guild and the midwife in the nursing home, Tressa persisted but kept hitting brick

_____

[6] This report does not include the full sequence of events but gives the pertinent details. A full report can be found at
https://www.irishexaminer.com/news/arid-20472276.html

walls. Twenty years later, she was eventually told that there was never an adoption order and that her son had been given to a family who had changed his name and date of birth.

André had no idea that he had been illegally registered until 2012 when he was fifty-two, and the adoption society tracked him down, telling him that his mother had been looking for him for about thirty years. The revelation that he was not the son of the people who had brought him up sent André into deep shock and changed his life forever.

I first spoke to Tressa by phone regarding her case when she was sixty-nine. I remember it well as she said, *'I'm nearly seventy now. I will never find my boy'*. I could not answer her for several minutes; such was her apparent anguish. André accompanied me to a meeting with the then Minister for Children, Frances Fitzgerald. At the start, André was being treated dismissively, but then he took the matter into his own hands and changed the course of the meeting. Standing up and placing his birth certificates on the table, he said, 'Can you tell me, Minister, why I have two birth certificates?' The Minister now had undeniable evidence of a falsified and illegal birth registration. In 2018, Tressa and André sued the State and the adoption agency for an undisclosed sum.

Mary's Story

Mary was another baby linked to Nurse Doody. She was born at St Jude's and was registered in her adoptive parents' names. She told me that when she and her 'mam' passed St Jude's on their frequent bus trips, her 'mam' would say, 'That's where I got you.

This is her account of how she came to be adopted as Mary Harris[7]

---

[7] Not her real name as she wishes her identity to remain protected.

Dr Coughlan approached my adoptive parents, asking them if they would consider adopting a baby who was due to be born in the coming weeks or months (I'm unclear). I was the baby. A little over a year later, he approached my adoptive parents for a second time, and they adopted a baby boy this time. We were born at St Jude's Nursing Home, Howth Rd, Raheny, Dublin 5. The owner/midwife was nurse Una Doody. Una Doody entered my adoptive parents' names into the St Jude's register as our birth parents, where Dr Coughlan was listed as the patient's doctor and Ms. Doody as the midwife. Then my adoptive father collected me from St Jude's a week after my birth.

My adoptive parents' names were entered on the birth certificate as birth parents. My adoptive father admitted that I was not his child at the time. Still, he pleaded with the registrar to enter his name as my father and my adoptive mother as my mother so that I would not grow up with the stigma of adoption/illegitimacy. After much discussion and arguing, the registrar agreed to the request, despite informing my adoptive parents that this practice was highly illegal and had been so since 1952.

When I was eight or nine years old, during a religion class, a nun was educating us about unwanted babies and the kindness of people who took them in and raised them. I was fascinated by the whole topic. The nun then said, "Hands up, all those adopted". I looked around to see four or five of my eighteen classmates had their hands up. I was shocked at how many had their hands up and felt so sorry for them for being 'unwanted'. I still remember making a mental note that I should be extra friendly and kind to them in the future. While I was still looking around, the nun said, "Mary Harris, put up your hand".

"Why?" I asked. I was genuinely confused.

"Because you're adopted."

I informed her that I certainly was not, but she persisted, demanding I put up my hand. When I was ordered to 'stand out, I refused, and an awful row ensued. The nun stormed down the aisle and tried to drag me from my seat, but I caught hold of the lid on my desk to anchor me and then held onto my friend when I thought she might succeed in pulling me away. I was fighting hard against her outrageous lie—as I thought it was. After that dreadful commotion, her parting comment was, "Ask your mother when you go home."

So convinced was I that she was wrong I actually forgot about it for the rest of the day. When my mother was kneeling by my bed saying our night-time prayers, I remembered what the nun told me to ask, so I did ... I never expected her to acknowledge that I was 'adopted'. And it got worse. All my friends on the road knew. I was the only one who didn't. My relationship with my adoptive parents broke down at that moment, and I never recovered. My confidence and self-esteem were completely and utterly shattered at that moment. I have never fully recovered or healed from the trauma.

From the age of twenty, I began actively searching for my mother. Dr Coughlan's son told me how he had gotten caught up in his father's illegal adoption activities when he finished college. He said his father had known it was illegal. Dr Coughlan had also blatantly lied to my adoptive brother and me, telling us we were birth brother and sister. This we now know not to be true.

Over the years, I rang the Adoption Board, Bernardo's, and any other organisation I thought may help, but to no avail. The mere mention of St Jude's ended the call swiftly. In 2009 I placed an ad on 'Adoptees Connect' stating, 'I am looking for my parents. I have little information to go on. I was born on Howth Road. I am female, short, dark-haired, sallow skinned'. I also gave my date of birth.

Unbelievably, my birth sister was scrolling on another linked site called 'Cousins Connect' when she came across my ad. Initially, we corresponded and exchanged photographs and phone calls. The likenesses in our appearance, lifestyle choices, and personalities are remarkable. I insisted on DNA testing with Cell Mark UK, which confirmed my mother/daughter relationship.

When my mother became pregnant with me, she was working for a well-known doctor. When she was due to deliver, he drove her over from the southside of Dublin to St Jude's Nursing Home. Immediately after my birth, I was wrapped in a white towel and taken away. My mother never saw me or got to hold me. She remained in St Jude's, drugged and locked in a room for a week.

When we eventually reunited after forty-seven years, she was surprised to hear that I may have been in the same building for most of that week. She had assumed my adoptive parents were waiting outside to take me home the moment I was born.

My mother returned to work for a doctor for a while, but when she became pregnant again, she fled to England, knowing if she stayed in Ireland, her child would also be taken from her. She married the father, and they had children together. Years after my birth, my mother returned to the doctor's home to find out where I was; in her own words, 'Things were not done right.

The task of finding me was difficult. My biological brother and sister drove out to the doctor's house looking for my birth and adoption records. His son answered the door and recalled my mother working there. He admitted to the files being there and said he would ask his father about retrieving them. But from that day, none of my sister's phone calls to the house were accepted. Eventually, my sister tracked the son down at his place of work when he informed her that the files had all been burned twelve months earlier.

On 18 March 2021, I took an Ancestry DNA test kit. Using this test, I found my first and second cousins, who connected me with my paternal family. I am in daily contact with four more siblings and numerous cousins. I've set up a 'Get to know my Facebook page and have spoken to my father by phone. They are all very accepting and welcoming, as was my maternal family.

To those not affected by adoption, on the outside, it all appears to be a happy ending. I have benefited enormously from finding my family, but I would be lying if I said the scars do not run deep. I constantly doubt my social and emotional skills, mainly about family.

Maura's Story

I was 19 when I was informed by relatives of my father that myself and my sister were adopted. My father had died a month previously, and my mother was on her deathbed in the hospital. The uncle who broke the news said that although all knew we had been adopted, none of the family knew the circumstances. We were (separately) illegally adopted. My birth cert states I was born at home to parents named mother and father, who I had believed all my life to be my birth parents. I had no reason to think or suspect otherwise, even though the family knew it, neighbours, even playmates, nobody spoke of it, not even hinted of it. Incredible.

It was like having the wind knocked out of you; everything you had taken for granted was turned upside down, but I couldn't think about it then; my "mother " was dying. She was in and out of consciousness, unable to speak following a stroke, but I remember seeing her the next day in the hospital. I brought flowers for her birthday. She knew I knew; what could I say? Nothing, I couldn't ask questions, she couldn't answer. She died two days later.

Over the next few months, I searched for any information on my birth. There was none; my birth certificate was falsified, and no records existed.

I was naive; I didn't know that the practice of illegal adoption was widespread; I never knew that pregnant girls and women were shamed and forced to give up their babies and baby homes or through other secret and discreet methods.

I convinced myself that I was better off, my birth mother didn't want me, and I was so lucky to have loving parents who chose me and kept my birth a secret to protect me so I wouldn't feel different.

As years went by, I got on with my life; the only real relevance for me was my lack of medical history. If I wondered about my birth mother and the circumstances of my birth, I knew the trail was cold; there was no way I could trace my origin, no paperwork, and no records existed. For a long time, I only gave it a passing thought, without much emotion, and then, it all changed,

Philomena

The heavens opened, the sky caved in, and my world turned upside down. Now I desperately must FIND MY MOTHER. Imagine what's going through my mind, was she forced to give me up? Have I lost her? Is it too late? Did she think about me and where I was? Was she trying to find me? I was devasted, tormented. People around me could not understand; how could they? I was grieving.

Now, I started to search again; I joined Facebook adoption groups, shared my story, and learned from others like me. I appealed for help through every possible channel. I made contact with old family, friends, and neighbours. I hoped that someone somewhere would know something but without success. It was hopeless.

Then it was Theresa who suggested I try DNA.

I knew very little about it and thought it was a long shot, but maybe my only shot was my last one.

The results were astounding! I was amused by my ethnicity results which indicated I was half Irish, half Italian! It had to be a mistake!

I had two close matches, 2nd cousins, with no connection to each other, so I had links to my parents! One of my matches contacted me, speculating how we might be related. I replied cautiously, worried I'd scare him off by saying I was adopted and trying to trace my family. He was not put off but revealed that he was a retired missionary priest and was keen to help if he could. At this stage, I have no idea if he was a maternal or parental match for me.

Meanwhile, I had contacted my other close match, from her profile, an American lady. She responded and was also keen to help when she understood my quest. She provided detailed information about her family returning to their original homeland, Ofena, Abruzzo, Italy.

I was also lucky to be contacted by another match in Ireland, a distant cousin with a passion for genealogy who was invaluable to me in my search. He created a tree from all my matches on both sides.

I found my father with Nicky, my Italian cousin, providing information. This opera singer had performed in cities worldwide, including Dublin, where he featured in the Dublin Grand Opera Society's Italian season at the Gaiety Theatre! I even found an advert in the Evening Herald for his appearance singing Tonio in Pagliacci 9 months before my birth.

My father, Paolo Silveri (1913 - 2001)

Back in Ireland, my cousin, Tom, was painstakingly putting my maternal matches in place. I was ecstatic when he told me he had narrowed the search down to 2 sisters, both of whom were still alive! Noreen and Rita are both unmarried and living together in Dublin.

My next move was to write letters to each, saying I was adopted and that I thought we might be closely related and said I would love to meet when I next came to Dublin.

I waited day after day for a reply, and I received a message from my 1st cousin, their nephew, stating, "we have read your letters with interest " and to contact him before my visit to arrange a meeting. Obviously, I think he wants to check me out to ensure I'm genuine.

To my surprise, when we arranged to meet 2 weeks later in Dublin's Talbot Hotel, he said he would be bringing Noreen with him (Rita was recovering in hospital from a broken pelvis sustained in a fall). I was a nervous wreck. Was I about to meet my mother or my aunt?

Noreen told me the story of how she travelled with Rita to a Northern Ireland "home" where Rita gave birth to me, unknown to any of their family. She was vague on details but said they knew the adoptive parents' identity and were briefly in contact. It also became clear that Rita had not yet seen my letter, so it was better to wait "for the right time" when she could receive the news at home.

That was in December 2018. I felt I was received warmly by Noreen and a bit more cautiously by her nephew. My visit to Dublin ended, and my wait continued.

In January 2019, I returned to Dublin to meet my birth mother. She knows about me, has read my letter, and is prepared to see me.

For me, the most important day in my 62 years; I'm excited, worried, terrified, and everything leads to this. Her first words to me were, "you're Maura; it's nearly your birthday, February" (my whole life, it's been a day out, the 17th). We sat together, Rita, Noreen, and myself, and it wasn't an easy conversation. Rita was unwilling to talk much about what was painful for her. She indicated that she didn't want anyone else in the family to be told, and she only expressed a passing interest in my life.

Nevertheless, although strained, I persisted with the meeting and let her take the lead. She and Noreen reminisced, and I tried to learn more about her life. No mention was made of her relationship with my father, who she referred to as "Silveri," although it seemed she and Noreen had travelled to see him in Rome.

It was agreed upon that I would return, and during that year, I went to Dublin to see her every couple of months whenever I could. Unfortunately, the meetings were always challenging; she insisted on maintaining secrecy, and I was not to meet my other cousins. On one occasion, when I asked how she felt about my reappearance in her life, she replied, "when you were born, I thought that was the end of it". I should have bit my tongue and said, " for me, it was just the beginning."

The meetings were interrupted in 2020 by Covid 19. With no travel possible and restrictions that carried on into 2021. The only communication I could have with Rita was by telephone. Those calls were short, impersonal, and strained, eventually leading to unanswered calls (I always phoned her). It was difficult and almost impossible to develop a relationship in these circumstances. A very worrying development over that time was when my cousin blocked me from his phone. I spoke to his wife, and her excuse was that he was not reacting well to the pandemic and not to be concerned. To this day, he still has not been in contact, and I am concerned. I think he is unhappy that I am my mother's only child and whether that has implications for him as her heir. Unfortunately, Covid 19 had more profound effects on me personally. I lost my business and have had to make significant changes in my life. My plans are uncertain, but up to now, I have still not been able to travel to Ireland. I do not know whether Rita will want to see me or if our brief reunion is at an end; it is a bitter disappointment for me to be rejected a second time, but I have to try again, and I just hope it's not too late. She is elderly and frail. It will have to be soon.

Recently Maura discovered that she was born in Northern Ireland, with her original birth records confirmed by Northern Ireland Direct. Legally registered in Belfast but trafficked to the south of Ireland, she was illegally registered as the biological child of Jeremiah and Teresa Griffin, the names of her adoptive parents.

The alienation adoptees feel when looking for what is, rightly theirs is catastrophic. After the initial excitement of meeting your biological family, it's like, what's next? what do you want? never fully understanding that what we are looking for is just an identity, to be accepted and to be part of the family structure with people who share your cultural heritage, that should have formed their early life. The unresolved grief over the lost relationship with birth parents is evident throughout their lives. In a closed or illegal adoption, there is no way for us to ask questions or clarify missing information, thus remaining in limbo throughout our lives. It feels like it is almost our fault and that, somehow, we should forget it and just get on with life. If only it were that simple.

My Mother's Story

Before I found my family, I had never been to Tipperary, so when I first visited the county, I was stunned by the spectacular views. While I was driving from the Dublin airport, especially when reaching a particular point known as the V. The curve in the road at a particular point offers a panoramic view over the countryside framed by the Knockmealdown mountains. I fell in love with the place instantly. However, my mother probably didn't see it like that.

From what I learned from my cousins, my mother, Alice Monica, was born on 4 August 1923. Very soon afterward, her mother died, and she was orphaned. She and her two brothers were sent to live with various family members who could give them a home. My mother was brought up by two unmarried aunts and an unmarried uncle on a farm in Co Tipperary. She was probably a joy in the lives of her two aunts—at least, I hope so. Ireland was full of unmarried men and women who were denied marriage because of the inheritance laws. At that time, the eldest son traditionally inherited the farm, leaving sisters and other brothers without any assets and unlikely to get married. The land monopoly and inheritance system encouraged arranged marriages to secure land consolidation. Women often had no choice of marriage partner and were perceived as belonging to their husbands. Sadly, a person's assets are more important than the person. It is not surprising, then, that women emigrated in droves after the famine to escape their humble role in an increasingly patriarchal society.

The farm was no place for a girl, and my mother's young years must have been dreary. No life, no fun. She once revealed how bitter she was because she spent her youth lonely and miserable. There is no doubt young women like my mother would have been expected to work hard and would not have had the benefit of running water (which was not available until the 1950s) for her household chores. My mother would have worked the land for many years with very few niceties for her to enjoy. Without receiving any land for dowry, she would not have been seen as a 'catch' for marriage in those days in rural Tipperary, and she was destined for a life of drudgery. What did she have to inherit after all her years of toil on her uncle's farm?

Nothing! He did, I believe, leave the farm to a nephew. How miserable she must have been. Tick. Tock. Tick. Tock. Time must have dragged by.

It is reputed that a local man who worked on the farm during harvesting was 'great' with her, meaning a dalliance was going on. At the end of the harvest, there were always grand celebrations. As had been happening for centuries, the ripened crops would have been harvested, which was a time for enjoyment. Traditionally, to celebrate a successful harvest, a party was thrown by the farmer for all the people who had worked and helped on the farm. This would be in the form of a dance, presumably a ceilidh (traditional Irish dancing), where the locals had a rare chance to let their hair down. It would have been a time when my mother and this lad could dance and enjoy themselves before he emigrated to Canada.

My mother, I believe, never saw him again, and it is possible that he never knew she was pregnant. Through DNA, I have established who my father probably is. I have a first cousin DNA match in Co Tipperary and an elderly uncle, his father, who is the only remaining brother. Unfortunately, the man I think is my father has passed away, having spent his life in Canada, but I believe I have four half-siblings.

As I presume it unfolded, the story was that my mother, on discovering she was pregnant, sought refuge in Dublin, where she would not be known. For single country girls who found themselves pregnant, the fear of meeting someone they knew, if they were to give birth in a local county home was so great that many chose to go to the city. This is what my mother chose to do. She perhaps had contact or a relative in Dublin who could point her in the direction of the people who were to make decisions about my life as I entered this world on 9th June 1954.

Dublin operated as an unofficial referral centre with places like the Catholic Protection and Rescue Society and the infamous St Patrick's Guild all involved in placing single mothers in institutions and sometimes employment. Unmarried mothers were sent to St Patrick's Home, Pelletstown, to one of the Magdalen asylums in the city, the Regina Coeli Hostel, or the Legion of Mary hostel, while Protestant girls went to the Bethany Home in Orwell Road, Rathgar. Protestant girls were also received at Pelletstown, but mothers preferred to be sent to homes that catered to their religious needs.

I assume my mother presented herself at the Coombe Hospital, where she acquainted Mareece Hannan, the almoner who set the wheels in motion for my 'adoption'.

I don't know where my mother stayed while in Dublin. Perhaps she was with a brother or other family member who lived there, but it must have been a lonely and distressing time for her. Returning to Tipperary shortly after my birth she continued with her life as though nothing had happened, and five years later, she married a farmer who was twenty years older than her. A kind man, I believe. They lived in a small cottage with a red door (which still stands today), and later they built a big house opposite. At last, she had a home of her own.

I was thrilled to hear that my mother had nine happy years with her husband. Nobody knew that she had had a child outside marriage, although there were rumours, and she could live a 'respectable', happy life. I have heard she was kind, very welcoming, and quite outspoken. She loved driving her friends through the hills of Tipperary in her Morris Minor. 'Get off the road! Mona Morrissey is coming!' was often a repeated comment. Not unlike me, I have to say! Strangely, I have always loved Morris Minors and have kept a miniature.

I agonized for years over what had happened to my mother. Did her family cast her out? Was she sent to a Magdalen laundry? I just hoped in my heart and soul that she went on to lead a happy life. That was my main concern. Once, before I found my mother, I wrote her a letter and sent it to various newspapers, hoping she would somehow come across it. Even if she did not act on it, she would know how I felt and that I did not blame her in any way.

To my birth mother

*I know it must have been difficult for you to hand over your baby ... but what choices did you have in the 50s? **None.** It must have been heart-breaking for you. I know as I have two children of my own ... grown up now ... and two beautiful little granddaughters. I cannot begin to imagine the pain you must have felt handing over your baby. I have been searching for you now for 14 years since I discovered I was adopted. I just want to know what happened to you and that you went on to have a happy life. I hope from the bottom of my heart that you did.*

How did my mother feel? I can't begin to imagine. No woman willingly gives up a baby and moves on with her life as if nothing has happened. Although I wasn't forcibly taken from her, the mores of the Irish society of the time forced her to give me up. She would have had no support financially, practically, or emotionally. I was two days old when she had to say goodbye to me. Two days old when I was handed over to strangers—people who were not part of my history. I was given to a woman who was incapable of love. I was doomed.

Ironically, it would all have been so different if I had been born eighteen years later. In 1973, unmarried mothers' benefits came into force, which allowed mothers to be financially independent. Contraception was finally legalized in 1985 after many protests by the feminist movement but was restricted and often impossible to acquire due to the still strict Catholic beliefs of many in the medical profession. The Catholic ethos enshrined in the constitution that it would take generations to change and be accepted. But at least there were now options available. I wouldn't have had to go through the nightmare of discovering the circumstances of my birth and the long, hard journey to find my mother.

Chapter 8
Ireland's Penal Colonies

Attitudes are not so easy to change, and Ireland's attitude to unmarried mothers did not change until well into the 1990s when single mothers began to be accepted. The shame heaped onto women who were pregnant and unmarried resulted in the perception that society had to get rid of them and they had to be hidden away. For over seven decades, they were labelled loose women, fallen women, whores, and criminals. And their baby would be given the derogatory label of bastard or illegitimate.

And so, in 1954, a female who found herself to be pregnant knew she had to hide away. She knew what could happen to her and her unborn child. Ireland had penal colonies—former workhouses turned into institutions under the guise of 'mother and baby homes.' From the 1930s to the end of the 1990s, an unmarried woman who fell pregnant was condemned to one of these places. But the name 'home' was a misnomer—homes provide comfort, support and kindness. But none of these were offered to the unfortunate women who were forced into these institutions by their families with the backing of the local priest. As these institutions were unregulated, those running them could impose their reign of terror. Who would have guessed that cruelty and incarceration could be interpreted as religion?

Adoption agencies opened across the country solely run by independent management boards comprising members of the clergy. In 1952, the new Adoption Act named legitimate but unmarried mothers as 'birth mothers'. Presumably at the instigation of those who wished to 'adopt' babies, to differentiate between the biological mother and the adoptive mother. There could be no mistake, only one mother could be known—and that was the woman rearing the baby. The biological mother had no say whatsoever and, in many cases, babies were illegally registered as being born to would-be parents. These cases, too, were sanctioned by those in authority.

A new market, an adoption market, was created with healthy babies – perfect babies – being the 'goods.' It was not only the clergy who supplied this new market. Those in close contact with the clergy – doctors, nurses and social workers and barristers, judges, solicitors and garda – all played a role in the trafficking of babies and young children. And it wasn't just the private mother and baby homes involved. (In fact, those who could afford to go to one of these homes were among the lucky ones.) The institutions run by the Catholic Church and financed by the State are just as culpable. It was a perfect crime, and the Catholic Church had a ready-made business.

Our society was well sought after by those from other countries simply because people could take advantage of the structure that allowed them to receive children to make their own. No one ever questioned the possible impact of this illegal practice on unsuspecting, innocent children (who would never know their heritage) or their mothers (who would never ever be able to trace their stolen child). With no adoption trail, many children simply vanished.

The shame and fear instilled in unmarried mothers rendered them too ashamed to talk about their experience, and therefore they would never search for their children. Many went to England to start a new life, never talking about the child they had been forced to give up. Traumatized by the treatment they had received in mother and baby homes and the loss of their baby; these women experience a living bereavement that continues for the rest of their lives.

The 'Boat to England' was a term used to describe the flight of thousands of pregnant, unmarried Irish girls who left their homeland searching for a solution. The Church was instrumental in forcing these girls, known as PFIs (pregnant from Ireland), to return to Ireland.

Frogmarched onto planes and then taken to a mother and baby institution, where they spent the rest of their confinement. Soon after giving birth their babies would be taken for 'adoption.' Interestingly it wasn't through kindness that they were brought back to Ireland, but because of the 'dangers' they would meet in Britain, the greatest danger being the indoctrination into the Protestant faith for the unborn child. In the UK, women had a better chance of making a life with their beloved children. The country was less judgemental, less of a closed society and, strangely, demonstrated stronger Christian values.

Incredibly, no one stepped in to help these girls who were being taken back to Ireland against their will. Where was either the police or the airport officials? It was probably presumed that the girls were criminals and who would argue with someone wearing the habit of a nun or the white collar of a priest? Terri Harrison was one of those women who is still heartbroken after being separated from her son, Niall. I once asked her, *"Did you not scream and shout?"*

"Yes, we did, but no one paid any attention."

Such was the power of those who wore the collar and the veil. Many 'adoptions' are facilitated by religious organisations who happily layer guilt on top of the trauma of relinquishment. I don't believe there is a god who wanted my mother and me to be parted, for me to be raised in secret by strangers and suffer lifelong trauma. If there is a god, I'd like to think compassion would be shown to mothers and their children.

None of the girls had committed a crime. However, in the eyes of the Catholic Church, they had committed the biggest crime of all by getting pregnant out of wedlock. They were denounced from the pulpit as sinners. They were scorned for their actions and the hurt they had caused God. Really? Many of the girls were pregnant due to serious crimes—rape, incest, and underage sexual intercourse. These crimes were never reported to the police or investigated. The nuns chose to ignore this information. To avoid denunciation and disgrace, the girl was banished by her family to one of the mother and baby institutions, which were nothing more than prisons, where she was kept until she gave birth. Their rights, their dignity, and their freedom were taken away. And ultimately, their beloved child.

In these institutions, the women were classed as inmates, stripped of their identities, and given new names. They were not permitted to make friends, although some did. Continuously subjected to humiliating treatment, such as cutting their hair and constantly being called 'fallen women' by the nuns, the women toiled like slaves from dawn to dusk without any pay, right to the point of giving birth. Constantly reminded that they had to pay for their sins. What sin? The sin of having sex and having a child out of wedlock. Condemned for giving birth outside marriage these women gave birth in agony with no pain relief, with the nuns sometimes whispering in her ear *'was the five minutes of pleasure worth it?*

June Goulding, a young midwife in the 1950s, worked at the Bessborough (Co Cork) mother and baby home run by the Sacred Heart Sisters. Her kindness and empathy must have been a welcome relief for many of the young women she encountered, as there was little in the way of pain relief or kindness and her experience of her time in the institution haunted her for years. She describes the cruelty of the nuns who oversaw the births, such as girls being forced to sit on a bedpan for hours. No antibiotic's administered when new mothers had infected breasts but were still forced to feed their babies.

If a woman's family could pay the one-hundred-pound release fee, she could leave soon after giving birth but without her baby. As any reference to her having had a baby would bring shame on the family, she was expected to continue with her life as though nothing had ever happened. It was never to be spoken about again. Those who could not afford the release fee, which was most of the women, had to stay at the home for at least twelve months to work off their debt for their so-called care. Some stayed for as long as three years or until their baby was adopted. Anthony Lee, the subject of the book, *The Lost Child of Philomena Lee* and the subsequent film *Philomena,* was almost four when he was taken for 'adoption.' This was the case for many of the girls. They would return to the nursery after a day's work only to discover that their baby had gone. What unimaginable cruelty.

One wonders why the nuns waited until the children were older. I presume that this was a deliberate act by the nuns to punish the women further, making them suffer even more for daring to engage in pre-marital sex—as though they had not suffered enough by being banished by their families and ostracised by society. What about the children who would have formed a very strong bond with their mothers by now? No thought was given to their feelings. By the age of three, most children would have a definite memory of their mother and would not understand why their mother had suddenly disappeared. The trauma of this separation can last right up to adulthood, and because traumatized children's brains are often wired for survival, as adults they function in survival mode, unable to feel part of the life, that they have been forced to live.

Many women have testified that they were coerced into signing a consent form after giving birth but were not told what they were signing. Most of these women neither fully recovered from their experience nor went on to have more children. There is anecdotal evidence that many were sterilized without their knowledge upon giving birth, totally unaware that they would never become mothers again.

No doubt my mother was aware of the notorious Sean Ross Abbey in her native Tipperary, and thank God, she chose another route. Under the 'Congregation of the Sacred Hearts and Jesus and Mary,' the abbey operated between 1931 and 1969. The report by the Commission of Investigation identified the cruel treatment handed out to young pregnant women and their babies in this institution. Survivors discovered as adults that they had been the subject of vaccine trials while they were there as infants. The records show that 6,414 pregnant women were interred over thirty-eight years. Of the 6079 babies delivered, one in six babies died, an extraordinarily high mortality rate.

As happened to many young women, my mother could have been stuck there for years. She understood she would never be allowed to be a mother to me, so she chose the illegal adoption route or was she aware of my fate? For her sake, I am glad she walked away. At least she had a life after me, for which I am truly grateful. I wish I had been given the opportunity to meet her as I'm sure it is from her that I inherited my stubborn nature. She must also have had a strong character. When she became pregnant, she was thirty years old, an intelligent and hard-working woman who the father of her child left. She surely did not have to be miserable for the rest of her life. Isn't having a baby in secret and having to give it away not enough suffering for one person?

What happened to the babies born in the mother and baby homes? Some babies would have been legally adopted, and many others would have been illegally adopted: 'adoptions' facilitated by the people society looked up to. Families adopted many babies in Ireland. But many became one of Banished Babies. (Irish children trafficked to the USA in the 1950s). Some children were placed in institutions at a very young age, staying there until they were sixteen, when it was no longer profitable for those running the homes to keep them. How many of these innocent children who should have been cared for by their mothers grew up in an institution? They would have been sad, lonely, perhaps abused and without support through no fault of their own. And the cycle continued.

Banished Babies

Who were the Banished Babies? The Irish State colluded with Church agencies to export 'illegitimate' children. This was effectively a black market whereby Irish babies were sold to rich American Catholic parents: child trafficking at its best. Archbishop McQuaid gave the nuns a moral dispensation to issue false birth certificates, leaving the babies untraceable by their birth mothers. The State issued passports for the babies who nuns accompanied to the U.S.A., where they were handed over to their new families. Ireland was decades behind Europe and America in proclaiming adequate legislation to regularise adoption, and thousands of babies were exiled, leaving behind grief-stricken mothers.

A story with the headline, '*1,000 children disappear from Ireland*' appeared in a German newspaper claiming that many babies and toddlers were destined for America to be sold for the price of three thousand dollars each, a princely sum back in the 1950s. '*American couples buy Irish babies through international adoption ring*' was the headline in an American paper. The article stated that the babies had come from private nursing homes around the country. Five of these were in Dublin. I could so easily have been one of those sent to the U.S.A!

An example of this is Anthony, the subject of the book and film *Philomena, who* was 'adopted' by a family in America. Having spent his formative years with his mother Philomena, he was taken and sent to America and renamed Martin Hess. What is so tragic is that both Anthony and Philomena searched for each other for decades, but the nuns refused to divulge any information. Today, there are adults in America who are still unaware of their illegal 'adoption'. In contrast others regularly appear on Facebook groups looking for information, all members of the Banished Babies support group, set up specifically for those trafficked from Ireland.

Who had the right to obliterate these babies' identities? Many babies just like Anthony were taken by Catholic organizations in Ireland and sold to wealthy American families who were unable to have children of their own. The Catholic Church has been accused of covering up the scandal, and many of the adoptees are still searching for the truth about their biological families. Their mothers would have assumed they had been legally adopted, but if the mother wanted to search for her child later in life, where would she start? There would be no records. And the adoptive parents would have been told that the mother had agreed to the 'adoption' or had died in childbirth.

My own mother may have assumed I had been legally adopted. Once I had been taken from her and 'sold on,' the problem was solved; she had no way of knowing where I had gone. Perhaps she did go looking for me when she got married, and this leaves me believing that my mother never knew what happened to me, and would never find out, a heart-breaking reality of which I may never know the truth.

PART 4: THE EMOTIONAL IMPACT

Chapter 9
The Perfect Solution?

In my view, regarding adoption as a perfect solution is a fallacy. It is an arrangement that creates a fictional family primarily for the sake of the adoptive parents, who are seeking the perfect family. If people could have their own biological children, I am sure there would be less demand for adoptions. People want the adopted child to look and act like them, but that, as we all know, is virtually impossible and unfair to the child. Adopting parents want the perfect child.

I know adopted people whose experience has been wonderful. They are loved unconditionally by their adoptive parents, and they lead happy lives. But I have also heard horror stories. One of the most controversial stories was in 2010 when a seven-year-old Russian boy an American family had adopted was sent back to Russia because of his behaviour. The adoptive parents felt that he was mentally unstable. What was not considered and probably never understood about the child's behaviour was that you can't just erase a child's memory. Adoption can bring joy and a sense of family to a child, but it also carries with it the responsibility of understanding a child's history and the potential for past trauma to manifest in behaviour This child was traumatized and subsequently ended up in an orphanage in Russia, experiencing further mental trauma. Would any parent do that to their natural child? I don't think so! The American adoption process was stopped by Russia because of this.

This was not an isolated case. Between one and five per cent of adoptions in the U.S.A are legally dissolved each year. This is a surprisingly high number considering adoptive parents go through rigorous screening processes and are expected to provide a stable home. Children who experience dissolved adoptions often experience further trauma, which can be difficult to overcome. There is even a website (WIAA) where these children are rehomed or offered 'second chance' adoptions, leaving it open to abuse. Imagine the psychological and emotional impact that this has on the child! No one would rehome their biological child if they didn't fit in. When will people stop thinking of children as commodities? Because of my own experience and the loss of my mother, my heart is full of sorrow for these defenceless children who should be loved and protected.

A biological child conceived by a couple will share their parents' DNA—their characteristics and appearance are influenced by genetics. Why, then, is the behaviour of adoptees and their characteristics constantly scrutinised? In my case, constantly hearing that I was the odd one out did nothing for my self-esteem, and I felt even more disconnected. The fact that you are different, even if you are the biological child, should not matter and comparisons are totally unfair. My two children are very different in character, but I love them equally. When I was growing up, I was never compared with other children academically, where I excelled. However, comparisons were made with the members of the family and my place within the family. I didn't fit in. They were not my tribe. Little did I know I could never be a part of it.

Although adoption might be considered better for children than placement in long-term foster or institutional care, there are some challenges adopted children face in overcoming the effects of early stress and the loss of their biological family. There is rarely acceptance or recognition of their original identity. These children are expected to fit into a family of strangers, spending a lifetime trying to be someone they are not. The lack of genetic connection between adoptive parents and the adoptee is rarely considered, nor is the recognition that biological heritage and identity are at the heart of what makes us human. Yes, people will always want a family, and the adoption process, if appropriately managed, can provide better outcomes for all involved. Always, of course, ensuring the child's welfare is paramount.

This is especially true for illegal adoptees because, unlike legal adoption, their whole existence is shrouded in secrecy. The child is placed in a new family and community and expected to accept it as home. Adoptive parents must be aware of these challenges and the eventual benefits they and the child will receive in terms of love. Perhaps adoptive parents should be monitored for a period of five years so that any issues can be identified early on. If you can fall totally in love with a stranger with all their faults, why not a child?

Very often, the adoptee's feelings are not considered; but they are expected to be grateful, living with unsolved grief for years. They constantly hear, '*You should be grateful and could have been in a home*. These were Kathleen's last words to me when I was looking for the truth. Not *We welcomed you. We loved you*, or *You were a joy to us*. None of these sentiments. In 2012 and 2013, the Australian government apologized to natural mothers and adopted people for past adoption practices. Although adopted people were mentioned in the apology, it was clear that the apology was meant largely for natural mothers.

The Emotional Impact on Adoptees

As a child, I always had a deep sense of loss that I could not understand or articulate. I felt an inexplicable void. I felt separated from everyone else by an invisible curtain. I could see children laughing, talking, and playing, but no matter how much I wanted to be on the same side, something stopped that from happening.

Something invisible was always there, but I had no idea what it was. I was different, the odd one. I guess I knew I didn't belong.

I have since discovered that the feelings of loss and rejection I experienced are real and linked to a condition known as 'attachment disorder.' This usually happens to children who have been separated from their biological parents/mother and children who have been neglected or abused. The effects last a lifetime. However, in 1954 these effects were never considered or known. Perhaps this is one of the reasons I was such a difficult and introverted child at times. God, if I had really known the truth.

It may surprise readers to hear that children grieve when separated from their mothers. Research has shown that any kind of loss of the familiar manifests itself in grief, and many adoptees say they have experienced this. Even those who had happy adoptions say that they always felt that something was missing. This is often called a "grief of origins" and can manifest in different ways, including insecurity, a deep longing for their biological family, or difficulty forming relationships.

Most people, especially those involved as adoptive parents, siblings, or relatives, are ignorant of this and just see it from the perspective that the adoptee has been given a nice home. The feeling of being given away perhaps evoked my own experience of feeling separate and different from everyone else. There was an emptiness inside like I was looking through a glass pane, not feeling part of anything. Having had countless encounters with other adoptees, it has become clear to me that this is a common emotion. Many have declared that they never really felt that they 'fitted' in.

'There is no such thing as just a baby. There is a baby and someone ...' is a well-known quote by Donald Winnicott.[8] By this, he means that a baby does not exist alone. What does exist is a 'nursing couple': an emotional, psychological, and spiritual unit of mother and baby within which knowledge comes from intuition and energy is exchanged. The baby and the mother, although separated physiologically at birth, are still psychologically one. Needless to say, this concept carries huge significance for children separated from their mothers at birth or soon after. Nancy Verrier, in her book *Primal Wound,* endorses this concept. The primal wound theory holds that 'severing the connection between the infant and biological mother ... often manifests in the sense of loss (depression), basic mistrust (anxiety) emotional and behavioural problems and difficulties in relationships with significant others. Nancy Vernier, in the same book, notes that established research reveals:

... bonding does not begin after birth but is a 'continuum of physiological, psychological and spiritual events beginning in utero and continuing throughout the post-natal bonding period. The interruption of this natural evolution, due to post-partum separation of mother and child creates a primal wound.

Spending forty weeks within your mother's body, close to her beating heart, ensures you have a common history and bonding with her even before you are born. The interruption of this bond has a profound effect on the child. The child does not experience just the loss of the mother but also a part of the self. That adoptees always search for their mother (rather than their father) clearly indicates that the strong connection with their mother cannot be severed and remains throughout life. Whether the severance happens a mere few

[8] https://www.cairn-int.info/article-E_JPE_010_0181--there-is-no-such-thing-as-a-baby-the.htm

minutes after birth or just a few days, the bond has been created: there is an unbreakable biological, genetic, historical, psychological as well as the emotional connection that can and should never be severed.

I know that the cells of my mother are part of me. I was never disconnected from my mother because during the nine months I shared her body, our cells mingled with mine slipping into her body and hers into mine: joined forever by our foetal cells. This process whereby mother and child harbour little parts of each other for eternity is known as foetal–maternal microchimeric. The mother lives the rest of her life with her baby's cells in her body. Cells from my mother (and possibly from my grandmother and my children) are knitted into my bones and brain; cellular threads bind families together in ways that scientists are just beginning to discover.

Is this why I (as, indeed, do other adoptees) always knew that something was missing? The never-ending void that was unexplainable until now. That our mothers never leave us.

Few people have the empathy to understand the level of grief that comes with the severing of genetic relationships, and the effects of the trauma experienced are not considered or taken seriously by family and friends. I remember discussing my distress at finding out about my 'adoption' with a neighbour in Rathfarnham. Her comment was, *"Everyone knew in Rathfarnham, but sure, it doesn't matter."*

Yes, it does matter.

It matters to me.

It matters to all those mothers who were prevented from being mothers to their children.

Ironically, people who make these comments are mothers themselves, but they don't stop to think about what it would be like for their child if that child were to be taken away forever. Perhaps it's because, in their eyes, single mothers still carry the stigma; they are one of the 'others.' Today there are still undertones of disdain for single mothers with various themes—such as receiving benefits and destroying the traditional family—being punted in the media.

"The separation of mother and child is always a trauma. Always. They experience their trauma at the exact same moment and is equally horrific for both".

Joe Soll and Jen Oakley

Adoptees and mothers who have lost their babies are expected to move on with their lives. Even though the trauma may have occurred decades ago, our psyche is permanently affected. This is perhaps why we are reluctant to talk about it. Thankfully, this is now being recognised and understood and is the reason for the many available support groups. However, many people searching DNA websites prove that people are obsessed with looking for family. Adoptees will always persist in looking for their mothers, it's the pull of genetics.

Finding Out About Adoption: The Emotional Fallout

For years I had been dealing with grief. But now, there were new emotions I had to deal with—discovering I was not who I thought I was and trying to adjust to my new reality had taken an enormous toll. Having spent forty-eight years believing I was a member of the family that 'adopted' me and then finding out that my reality was totally different has left scars and confusion. I dip in and out of my new family's lives but still know Margaret and Bernie as my sisters. I'm an amalgam of two families, a hybrid human. I still feel that I don't belong fully to either family, mainly because of the passage of time, and there is nothing anyone can do to improve it. The scar tissue persists. That's the heart-breaking reality of the lies and deceit I have

105

been living with for the past sixty-eight years. A lifetime of suffering that does not end. No one wins in this type of arrangement. Not the adoptive parents, not the birth mother and certainly not the adoptee. For the adoptee, that 'primal wound' never heals. It remains like a festering wound, ready to open at any time.

During the first two years after finding out about my 'adoption', I constantly looked in windows and mirrors, wondering who I really looked like. I constantly looked at women in the street, seeing resemblances that were not there. Not knowing who I was the strangest feeling ever. I felt I was in limbo, and from waking until going to sleep at night, my thoughts dwelt on what I had found out. Had my mother tortured herself with the same thoughts, I wondered. When she encountered children of different ages, did she wonder whether that child could be hers, her emotional wound opening every time, never to heal?

How extraordinary that it took forty-eight years to make sense of it all. But then why would I? Don't you trust your parents and family? That trust is a reliance on another person, especially a parent, and once violated, it provokes disappointment and an ongoing feeling of betrayal.

Other adoptees have expressed the profound emotional impact of being adopted:

Every area of my life has been affected by what I have discovered. I have great problems trusting people – both friends and men – and once I do trust someone, I seem to find it hard to say goodbye, even if the relationship is really rubbish. Taking time to do a degree in psychology, philosophy and sociology has helped me look at why individuals do things. It does not in any way excuse their behaviour but offers insight to make sense of it.

106

The thing I remember most about the day I discovered that my adoptive mother didn't give birth to me was this feeling of being in a tunnel going round and round, trying to latch on to reality. Elated in one way that we were not biologically related, however, the reality of what I was experiencing became a nightmare. Everything I had known to be true was a lie, and I no longer knew who I was. After all, she was the only 'mother' I knew, and I had accepted a long time ago that there was just no bond. Well, yes, I guess I was right there. Not even a whisper.

I felt very angry with my adoptive mother about the web of deception for a long time, and although I've worked through that now, I still strongly believe that people have a fundamental right to know about their origins. Whether one considers their adoption in a positive or negative light is really neither here nor there. The damage remains the same. The harm remains the same. My identity was erased all the same.

The Emotional Impact on Mothers

In *Women Who Run with The Wolves*, Clarissa Pinkola Estés writes, 'Any society that forces women to give up their own flesh and blood to conform to its norms is a sick society indeed!'

All women reading this who have experienced the joy of holding their baby will agree that it is the most wonderful feeling in the world. There is the intense desire to protect this little human you have given life to. Out of nowhere comes the primal urge to protect. Now close your eyes and imagine your beautiful child being torn from your arms, and you have no say in the matter. Think of the everlasting pain and grief you would feel. This has been the experience of thousands of women.

The mother can grieve if a child is stillborn or dies after birth. There are announcements of death and accepted rituals that permit her to express her emotions. Friends and family members gather to support her. This does not happen with adoption. There is just silence. There is no announcement of either the baby's birth or loss. There is no family to support these grieving mothers who must hide their feelings as they did during their pregnancy. There is no recognition of a 'mother' because there is no baby, except in whispers. The silence is all pervasive and is interpreted as an expression of disapproval. How heart-breaking for a new mother. The loss or, indeed, the mother's grief is not recognised. Mothers suffer in silence, and the child experiences an unexplained loss. Both experience a lifetime of bereavement. How many mothers, I wonder, unknowingly suffered post-natal depression, and never recovered? I know my mother suffered, as confirmed by someone who knew her well.

The assumption that adoptees are privileged as they will have a better life is a fallacy. Adoptive parents rarely feel privileged to have that child in their life. They feel that it is their right and no consideration is given to the birth mother—the woman who carried that child for nine months, who felt its first movements and, indeed, heard its first cry. That mother who is now living a life of bereavement. I say 'real mother' here because that is exactly what she will always be. You don't become an ex-mother. You are forever the mother who could not keep your baby through circumstances beyond your control. You are fragmented and broken. Never the same again. 'Move on.' You'll have other children is the coldest, most inconsiderate comment a mother who has lost her child will hear.

Had our mothers had the support they should have; I and many others would have lived a different life without the experience of empty space in our souls. That it is unnatural for a child to be separated from its mother and presumed to be part of an adoptive family is illustrated in countries that practice Islamic Law. The artificial creation of family ties is considered to be impossible, and adoption is outlawed in most countries under Islamic rule. *Kafala* is a form of guardianship with no family ties being created between the child and guardians, thereby preserving the child's heritage and identity. The only stipulation is that the guardians must be of the Muslim faith.

My situation robbed me of the right to be raised by my mother, to be raised around and share history with my family. But more than that, the secrecy and lies have robbed me of time. I could have shared the time with my mother before her death in 2009. The time that I will never get back.

PART 5: CULPABILITY

Chapter 10
What History Tells Us Background

Weaving its way through the pages of this book is our history—the history of Ireland, the politicians; the Catholic Church; and all the people of Ireland. What follows next is not a definitive history of Ireland: it is a personal interpretation of how the events damaged my mother, me, and many others. My sources are books, school lessons, personal interviews and the passed-down narratives that are the fabric of Irish people's lives.

Hiding pregnancies and babies is not new. The Foundling Hospital in Dublin was opened in 1704, with its two objectives being to avoid the deaths and murders of illegitimate children and to teach the Protestant faith to the children. 'Professional lifters,' as they were called, were paid to remove unwanted babies from people living in Dublin parishes and much further afield in countryside locations. Under cover of darkness, the lifters carried the babies, often up to eight infants in a bag, to the Foundling Hospital (now St James' Hospital).

However, the mortality rate of the babies was alarmingly high, and none of the children were educated. As far back as 1758, a report to the Irish House of Commons outlined the deplorable conditions in the Foundling Hospital. Lady Arabella Denny from Blackrock, Co Dublin, who was economically privileged and a Protestant, had a compassionate heart and sound moral values. Disgusted by the conditions described in the report, took over the running of the hospital, training nurses and improving the care of the infants. Along with donating her own money to the cause, she established a system of donations, raising much needed funds to modernize the hospital and increase its capacity.

Lady Arabella's work transformed the hospital, and it became a model of excellence in the care of infants. She is remembered today as a champion of the vulnerable and a beacon of hope for those who need it most.

During the ten years between 1760 and 1770, of the 8,726 infants in the nursery, 6,721 survived, and only 1,990 died. Previously, four out of five babies died. What an outcome when love and care are involved!

This kind woman was moved by the outpouring of grief from women who did not know what had happened to their babies. Their experiences were detailed in letters written by farm girls, servants, and women from the city. Their station in life was unimportant: all were desperate to know what had happened to their infants. Lady Arabella went on to open the first Magdalen Home in Lower Leeson Street in 1767. Entry to the home was voluntary, and women were not forced to stay there. Those who were admitted ranged in age from twelve to thirty and were taught new skills to enable them to seek employment. On leaving, they were given money to help them start a new life. Is this not a Christian attitude? Lady Arabella was a Protestant, raising the question of whether life, particularly for women, under British rule would have been better than under Catholic rule. I know how I may have answered the question had I been asked.

When Lady Arabella died in 1792, Peg Leeson, Dublin's most famous Madam, closed her brothel as a sign of respect. She had secretly funded the Magdalen Home for many years, although very few who entered the Magdalen were prostitutes. Eventually, the Magdalen Home moved to Eglington Road, Dublin, and was renamed Denny House. Lady Arabella's vision to help and support women who had unwanted pregnancies and lost their babies was not to last, unfortunately, as history has shown.

Ireland Under British Rule

The collective memory of the British in Ireland remains a bitter one. In the mid-1840s, people were starving and had been dispossessed of their property by the English landlords. It is not surprising that the population declined dramatically between 1844 and 1851. This was due to about one million people dying and approximately two million emigrating, deeming this their only option. Ireland's population depletion is seen as a tragic consequence of English rule, and the seed of hate was sown.

An unforeseen and unfortunate consequence was that this hate of the English unknowingly created a staunch Catholic identity. The Irish were keen to achieve independence from the British rule they had been under for centuries and saw Catholicism as a symbol of that independence. After independence, Irish Catholicism emerged as an extremely strong institution that wielded significant power for decades –to the detriment of women.

1922: The Free State

Irish women were strong, respected, and active during the nineteenth and twentieth centuries. They were politically engaged in nationalist and women's organisations and had played an important part in the fight for Irish independence in the Easter Rising of 1916, the War of Independence (1919–1921) and the civil war of 1922–1923. Under the Proclamation of 1916, both men and women were granted equal citizenship.

As described atthe beginning of this book, after eight hundred years of English rule, in 1922, the Irish Republic was formed. In June 1922, the Constitution of the Free State was drafted. It set out the rights and freedoms of citizens of the country and separated Church and State. All Irish citizens over the age of twenty-one, regardless of sex, were enfranchised under the Free State Constitution of June 1922, for which women had strongly lobbied. They were in an ideal position to benefit from their role in the fight for Irish Freedom.

Their newfound rights, however, were soon to be eroded. The ideals of 1916 would not be restored until almost fifty years later, when an emerging generation of feminists and advocates transformed a society where everyone is treated equally regardless of their sex.

1929: Censorship of Publications Act

The first indication of women's status being eroded came in 1929 when the Censorship of Publications Act was passed. The Act aimed to protect societies morals by prohibiting the publication of material deemed indecent or immoral. The prohibition of contraceptive advertising was the start of control over women. Contraception was finally legalized in 1985 after many protests by the feminist movement, and even then, it was restricted, and contraceptives were often impossible to acquire due to the still strict Catholic beliefs of many in the medical profession. In the 1990s, contraceptives were increasingly available and finally, in 2015, the Government passed a law that allowed women to access contraceptives without medical prescription. This marked an important step towards gender equality as women finally had access to the same health services as men. The Catholic ethos was so enshrined in the constitution that it would take generations for contraception to be accepted.

1937: The New Constitution

In 1934, Eamon de Valera constituted a four-person committee to examine the 1922 Constitution, and in 1936, the drafting of the new constitution commenced. The new Constitution of 1937 was ratified by the people in a referendum and took effect on 29th December of the same year. It was ultimately replaced by the Bunreacht hEireann (the Irish constitution) in 1937.However, much of the discussion took place behind closed doors. It was only when the constitution's final draft was published in 1937 that it became abundantly apparent that the government was not prepared to take women and their rights seriously.

The phrase '... regardless of sex ...' in the 1922 constitution had been removed. Further, the role of women was now being curtailed. They were described as the weaker sex, and the women's role was to be in the home and care for their children. Women were not allowed to vote, nor did they have access to education or job opportunities. Women were largely excluded from the public sphere, and their rights were subordinated to those of men. This idea was reflected in the laws and official documents of the time. Women were not allowed to vote, own property, or have the same rights as men.

There was fierce opposition from women to this. The journalist, Gertrude Gaffney, responded to the draft constitution in her column in the *Irish Independent*: 'Mr de Valera has always been a reactionary where women are concerned. He dislikes and distrusts us as a sex, and his aim ever since he came into office has been to put us into what he considers our place and keep us there.' Hanna Sheehy Skeffington wrote to the *Irish Independent* that the rights guaranteed to all citizens in the 1916 proclamation were being scrapped for a fascist model in which women would be relegated to permanent inferiority because they were 'the weaker sex. [9]

Church—State Interdependence

Much has been written about the role of the Catholic hierarchy in advising de Valera on the constitution, and the awesome power of Cardinal McQuaid in Ireland between December 1940 and January 1972 is well known. It is clear the Catholic hierarchy played a significant role in advising de Valera on the constitution, as well as in influencing public opinion during the time period when McQuaid was the leader of the Catholic Church in Ireland.

The publication of the de Valera papers relating to the drafting of the 1937 constitution shows the extent of McQuaid's power and how McQuaid collaborated closely with de Valera in drafting the law of the State. It is clear that McQuaid's influence was far-reaching, and he was able to shape the course of the Irish state for decades to come. Under the new constitution in 1937, a special place was given to the Church as 'head of Irish society'. Due to its organisation's strength and with backup from Rome, the Church could influence what Irish people said and did, maintaining control over morality issues regardless of whether Irish people were committed to the Church. In reality Church and State were the same thing. McQuaid and President de Valera, working in unison, ruled with an iron fist, controlling people's lives for decades by instilling fear and relying on a submissive population.

[9] Maria Luddy, 2015, A 'Sinister and retrogressive' Proposal: Irish Women's Opposition to the 1973 Draft Constitution. *Transactions of the Royal Historical Society,* Vol 15 (2005) pp 175–195.

At that time, the country's administration was divided between the Church and the State: the financially depleted government was responsible for developing the country, while the Church took responsibility for schools, hospitals, and other social services. Increasingly, McQuaid distrusted foreign ways and was adept at harnessing State resources for social and educational initiatives that were run solely by the clergy or other Catholic organisations. The ideas of liberal thinkers in *The Irish Times* offices, Trinity College or the Communist Party were curtailed. McQuaid rejected any form of progressive thought, even in education and banned the teaching of John Dewey, Maria Montessori and others that were being welcomed in developed societies. There was no way that the Irish people could be allowed to think for themselves!

He was determined to keep the people in a state of ignorance and poverty, as it was easier for him to control them. His policies had a lasting impact on the Irish people, whose educational opportunities were significantly restricted. When McQuaid's archive was opened in 1997, it revealed the presence of an unsophisticated spy system that the FBI admired. This was the stuff of a dictatorship intended to keep Irelands people suppressed by organizing medical, legal, and teaching professions along with government departments. It opposed compulsory school attendance for primary school pupils, destining these young children to work from a very young age.

The Church also had a heavy hand in the media, censoring any criticism of their rule. McQuaid's archive revealed how the Church's grip in Ireland was so strong that they were able to maintain control of the population for decades. McQuaid's archive was instrumental in exposing the truth about the Church's oppressive rule. However, this ultimately led to a wave of social reform in Ireland, including the legalisation of compulsory attendance in primary schools.

It could be said that the Church stepped in to offer services such as health and education in the newly formed State, without which the people would have been without schools and hospitals. While there may be an element of truth in this perspective, because of the conditions in the early nineteenth century, it is not correct. The Church consistently undermined State services and the State's progression and put its own power ahead of the needs of vulnerable people. The Church was also guilty of placing its own interests above those of the people, for example by maintaining a hold on education and health services. This stifled the potential for progress and prevented the vulnerable from accessing necessary services. The Church's control and involvement in our State systems were not motivated by charity but by power.

The Church became intimately involved in family life. It preached the importance of marriage and the family and that the only justifiable reason to have sex was for procreation. Beyond that, the act was considered to be evil. The confessional provided a great source of information for the local priest, giving him detailed knowledge and providing scrutiny of people's intimate details and behaviour. Sunday after Sunday, from the pulpit, priests would spew forth their tirades against unmarried pregnant women and their 'unspeakable sinfulness.'

Women in 1950s and 1960s Ireland

In Ireland in the 1950s and 1960s, women lived in a society that was completely dominated by the Catholic Church's teaching. From the time they started primary school, children were exposed to the teaching of the Church and absorbed the teaching as irrefutable. Contraception was forbidden, and women were prevented from working. They were led to believe that bringing up children in the

118

Catholic faith was their most important role in society, confining women to the home. Women who conformed to this ideal earned respect and status that they could not otherwise have expected. As illegitimacy carried such a stigma, virginity became highly esteemed in young girls. The Blessed Virgin (who became pregnant outside marriage—conveniently overlooked by the sanctimonious priests) was the ultimate role model. With now huge devotion to Our Lady, every family had a Mary. Girls were brainwashed and indoctrinated from a very young age, making it so easy to shame girls when they committed the sin of all sins: having sex. Women began to face terror if they became pregnant outside of marriage.

The Church's overwhelming influence on Irish society contributed to the brutal way women were treated. In fact, it is difficult to understand in the progressive Ireland of today how entangled the State was with the Church and how together they controlled and brainwashed citizens. Blurring boundaries between the State and Church allowed a State-sanctioned misogynistic culture. President de Valera, when introducing the Constitution in his speech to the Dáil, acknowledged stripping the principle of equality away because, he said, women needed to be protected. But not all women, as evidence suggests. Perhaps he meant married women under the guise of 'respectability.' Certainly not the 'fallen' women who were taken advantage of and looked down on by society. There were few options for women and much to fear; such was the power of the Church. Going against the consensus of the time was dangerous and could result in loss of job, social isolation and, for many Irish women and their babies, their lives could be exacerbated. For these women, there was little chance of justice or escape from the grasp of the Church. Many lived in poverty and had to face the consequences of their 'transgression' alone. Society at the time had no empathy for their plight.

Single Mothers

With no provision to help single mothers, those in the Church, enjoying their power, came down hard on these vulnerable women. The papal encyclical *Casti Connubii (chaste wedlock)* made sure of that. Before the encyclical was issued in 1931, the clergy were horrified to find that the social tendency of the day was to support single mothers. Things would have to change, and a statement was issued:

We are sorry to note that not infrequently nowadays it happens that through a certain inversion of the true order of things, ready and bountiful assistance is provided for the unmarried mother and her illegitimate offspring ... which is denied to legitimate mothers or given sparingly or grudgingly.

This was cruelly aimed at single mothers, inferring that the help they were getting was at a cost to married mothers. Not surprising; therefore, that Irish society was reluctant to offer support to those who, Rome now persuaded them, were immoral women.

In the early 1950s, Dr Noel Browne, the then Minister of Health, proposed providing free access to health care for mothers and children as the absence of antenatal care resulted in high fatality rates. He aimed to tackle unacceptable levels of child mortality by introducing free ante-and post-natal care for mothers and extending free health treatment for all children under 16 without a means test. But he was opposed by GPs concerned their incomes might be threatened, and colleagues in government who were probably under pressure from the Catholic church.

The mother and child scheme was mooted. However, McQuaid strongly opposed the scheme, claiming that it was against the moral teaching of the Church. His strong political influence prevailed, and the government withdrew the scheme, which would have saved countless lives and benefited mothers. At the root of their opposition was the perception that Browne's scheme would open the way to liberal family planning and contraception and, of course, the Church would slowly lose its power, not to mention the income generated by illegitimate babies destined for adoption and trafficked abroad for a heavy fee which went straight into the church's coffers. Under pressure from bishops, the coalition government at the time backed away from the scheme forcing Dr Browne's' resignation on 11th April 1951 as Minister for Health

What developed country would put its citizens in so much obvious danger? This reflected the Irish government's weakness in challenging the Catholic Church's authority. How different things would have been if Dr Noel Browne's proposal had gone ahead. Mothers would not have died, and children would not have been orphaned.

I would not be writing this book.

Mother and Baby Homes

Illegitimate children had no rights, and neither had their mothers. The shame of being an unmarried mother in Ireland in the 1950s was extreme, and there were few options for women back then. They could expect absolutely no support. However, the Catholic Church was on hand—at a price. With the full knowledge of the State, women were routinely incarcerated in homes and institutions and had to relinquish their children for adoption before they were released. They were given no option. They could not keep their child. The most common response to illegitimacy was silence, never again to be talked about, which enabled decades of secrecy. Decades of silence and secrecy allowed for the abuse and mistreatment to go unchecked. This led to a culture of impunity, where the perpetrators of abuse were never held accountable.

The government, along with the Roman Catholic and Protestant churches, ran institutions cruelly and without compassion. The misery these women endured surely could only happen under a political dictatorship.

However, it should not be forgotten that the nuns, who watched their charges' every move, were conforming to the demands of Irish society. The nuns, too, lived in a repressive patriarchy with few options for women. Some may have experienced a spiritual calling as young girls, but others would have opted for the religious life rather than becoming a farmer's wife and having to be at their husband's beck and call, overworked and pregnant year after year. Most of the young women who became nuns came from rural areas and been boarders at their secondary schools for several years. They would have no idea about sex and so easily persuaded by the narrative that women who had sex outside marriage were fallen, women. The nuns were taught that the only way to avoid such a fate was to remain celibate and devote their lives to God. They were made to believe that sex was something to be feared and avoided at all costs. This encouraged them to remain in the convent and serve God.

It was easy to dominate these institutionalized women, and it would have been impossible to expose this violence beyond the walls of their institutions. There could be an element of jealousy: these young nuns who had taken vows of chastity may subconsciously have wanted a sexual relationship and to become a mother.

Within the institutions, however, nobody could escape the interlaced structure of these complex power relations. The nuns took vows of poverty, chastity, and obedience, but compassion was not one that was asked of them. I believe cruelty is not learned. It's there, just waiting to emerge at the right moment—or at the wrong moment for the victim. When empathy is eroded, it is easy to see people as less than human. Encouraged by a sheer lack of empathy and compassion, the nuns, who had sadism as part of their psyches, had the perfect job. They took pleasure in inflicting suffering on a vulnerable person who was at their mercy. The most vulnerable were the young unmarried mothers, abandoned by their fathers and, in many cases, their families, who had their babies in these institutions. How lonely it must have been for them when giving birth to a child should be a happy occasion. Instead of feeling joy, they were made to feel shame.

Tens of thousands of women were punished for bringing shame on themselves and their families. They were banished to these institutions to atone for their sins, working long hours without pay. Gertrude Gaffney, the Irish journalist, and advocate of women's rights published a series of articles in 1936 about Irish women in England. One such article, *Unchristian attitude of parents,* described how priests, nuns and lay people who were connected with rescue work in London spoke of the unchristian and inhuman attitude to unmarried mothers in Ireland, making life more difficult for the women and harder for them ever to make good. This article highlighted the plight of Irish women in England and the need to address the issue with urgency. Gaffney's articles were instrumental in bringing attention to the issue and sparking a debate in the Irish public sphere. Parents trusted and feared the Church, so they handed over their daughters without question to eliminate the problem. How arrogant and sad to have your family dictated to by Rome.

First-time mothers were described as 'first-time offenders' who could be rehabilitated in a mother and baby home, whereas it was considered doubtful that mothers who had given birth a second or third time were capable of rehabilitation. This term was used for many decades concerning unmarried mothers, even used in 'Chains or Change'—the manifesto of the Irish Women's Liberation Movement. The use of 'rehabilitation' and 'first offenders' denoted criminality on the part of unmarried mothers, and references to women tended to be framed in indirect language. The women were denied their humanity, and their voices were always absent.

The easy answer would have been, of course, the use of contraceptives. However, as contraception was strictly forbidden in Catholic teaching, this was never an option. Once again, people's lives were dictated by Rome.

'We are dealing with a crime that is committed nearly every hour and certainly every day of the week.' This statement by Sharon O Halloran, director of Safe Ireland (domestic abuse) in 2012, could just as easily have been a reference to what happened to women in these institutions. There was violence against women, but unlike domestic abuse victims, they had no one to hear them. They had no voice. There was no group to advocate on their behalf. How different things might have been if the abuse had not been hidden behind closed doors by the Church and State. Yes, the needs of vulnerable people (like unmarried mothers who were cast aside in society and incarcerated, depriving these girls of their legal and constitutional rights) were not met.

In Ireland, the Church's authority was unquestioned and those in the Church were deemed infallible. Institutions such as the mother and baby homes, which were run by religious orders, had a veil around them, and a blind eye was turned to the treatment meted out. Because of the shame they felt, women were reluctant to reveal to others what they had been through or were too embarrassed to talk about their past. They never told a living soul about their horrific experience. This has led to the perpetuation of a culture of silence, where survivors of these homes have been unable to speak out and seek justice. A legacy of trauma has been created and passed down through generations which still affects many today.

The Church and society were complicit in propping up this cruel system, but ultimately the buck stopped with the State. Instead of protecting its women and children, the State permitted the treatment to continue for decades.

Chapter 11
Exposure

Despite the Irish Adoption Bill coming into force in 1952, illegal adoptions continued for many more years. The mother and baby homes, where unmarried pregnant women were admitted, were mainly run by nurses, many of whom were involved in this informal or illegal adoption practice. In 1972, when the new Health Act came into force, by an astounding coincidence, forty-two such homes closed. Even more astounding and statistically unrealistic is that no files are available from these homes. Eventually, in 2011 a file was found in Ms. Doody's attic. She had been a nurse working and residing in St Jude's home on Howth Road, Dublin. The file contained records of a thousand birth registrations from 1938 to 1968, both legal and illegal. Where are all the other files? They surely exist and are hidden somewhere. All those who have been illegally adopted or registered have a right to access them.

During all the years I have researched illegal adoptions, I have yet to find one where money was not involved. How was it possible for this lucrative business to start (I use the word 'lucrative' deliberately as there was always money involved)? Children could be regarded as commodities as there were plenty of babies available: birth control was prohibited by the Catholic Church, and options were limited for those who opted to disregard the directive. The cultural norms of the time allowed the practice to thrive. The level of financial advantage to be obtained by the sale and purchase of children was a major factor driving illegal adoptions. While the ethics of professionals flouting the law is disturbing in the extreme, even more disturbing is the systemic, government-sanctioned practices that were overlooked and the constant silence that people face trying to find the truth, their origins, their identity, like me, are met with when approaching the Irish State.

Those involved in the illegal registrations have justified their actions by claiming they feared the children would face the stigma of adoption. Although there may be an element of truth in this, it's a very tiny element. The process offered hope to couples who could not conceive their own child. It was a way of secretly acquiring a permanent family and hiding infertility, which carried huge stigma and shame in Ireland in the 1950s and 1960s.

Many of the people from around the country who were illegally adopted admitted indescribable shock at finding out only when they were in their sixties that they weren't who they thought they were. Over 180 organisations and private individuals arranged adoptions, many of which were also involved in facilitating illegal adoptions, yet very few of these files have ever been handed over to the State. I can imagine that there are probably thousands of people out there who are unaware that they have been illegally adopted/registered.

And what about their medical background? Most families, with their common genetic background, will have information about conditions that run in the family. These could be traced back as far as three generations. Doctors can determine if an individual, family member, or future generations may be at risk of developing a serious condition. Knowledge of family history allows a person to take steps to reduce their risk. This can be done through regular check-ups, lifestyle changes and preventative measures, or even through genetic testing. Knowing family history can also enable individuals to make better-informed decisions about their and their family's future health. But of course, adoptees, especially illegal adoptees, are ignorant of any of these health risks. Many of the people I have spoken to over the years cite the lack of medical records as a major concern, with no clues to genetic diseases and it is impossible to predict.

As I write this book, however, legislation in Ireland changse on 3rd October 2022. Due to this new legislation, every adoptee, illegally registered, boarded out or fostered, will gain the right to unredacted files. is has been a long time in coming; Many of the people affected by this legislation have waited years to access their records. This new law marks a significant milestone in the Irish adoption system and will be a major step forward in providing adoptees with the information they need to connect with their past and their biological families. It will also help to ensure that all adoptees have access to their personal records in the future. This has been a long time in coming; in fact, it has taken decades, and the change in legislation is due to the various activist groups campaigning for what is their right, their birth files.

The new legislation will release the person's birth certificate, medical background, and information about their early life. The information will be provided whether the mother or genetic relative's object. It will also include releasing baptismal certificates and copies of entries in the parish baptism register. There is anecdotal evidence that in the case of illegally registered children, there were two birth certificates, one with false details much like their birth certificate and another one said to be kept in a register at the Archbishop's house.

In Ireland, before getting married, couples must apply to their parish priest for a letter of freedom, ensuring they were not married previously. Searching in the archives for baptismal certificates would identify if there were two. This was to ensure that couples did not marry their sibling. It makes one wonder how this would be explained to an unsuspecting couple if it arises. Access to this information for illegally registered people may hopefully provide more information.

In line with this, a comprehensive statutory tracing service will be set up for anyone who wishes to make contact, share, or seek information about their birth and early life. This will be in the form of a Contact Preference Register, which will allow people to register their preference for contact with family.

Pulling the First Thread

In 1998, the last mother-and-baby home closed its doors. Then in 2012, Catherine Corless, an amateur historian, published an article about a mother and baby home near Tuam, Co Galway, owned by the local council and run by the Bon Secours Sisters. Catherine questioned the high number of infant deaths in the home and the lack of records between 1925 and 1961. In 2014, she went public with her conviction that as many as 800 babies could be buried in a septic tank at this mother-and-baby home. The international outcry that followed forced the government to act, and in February 2015, a commission to investigate the claim was set up. Judge Yvonne Murphy was appointed as the chairperson, and Professor Mary E. Daly and Dr William Duncan as members. Initially, they were given three years to complete the entire report, but after several extensions had been granted, it eventually took six years.

The Commission of Investigation

The proposed Terms of Reference for the 'Commission of Investigation into the Mother and Baby Homes and other related matters' was published by Mr. James Reilly TD in 2015 when he was the Minister for Children and Youth Affairs. Under the umbrella of CMABS (Coalition of Mother and Baby Homes Survivors), we had a meeting with the Minister prior to the publication, and each group submitted their proposals. We felt that, at last, there was someone who was listening. My interest, of course, lay in illegal adoptees and my questions were as follows:

- Even though the Irish Adoption Bill came into force in 1952, illegal adoptions continued until the late 1980s. In 1972, forty-two mother and baby homes closed suddenly, mainly run by nurses involved in this illegal practice. How many of these were inspected as required by law under the 1934 Registration of Maternity Homes Act? The Act also amends the Succession Act 1965 to address inheritance issues arising for people affected by illegal birth registration.

- Why was St Rita's allowed to continue to operate as a mother and baby home when it was well-known that Mary Keating was involved in illegal adoptions?

- How was St Jude's nursing home on Howth Road allowed to operate and facilitate illegal adoptions if it was inspected under the 1934 Act?

- The former Minister for Children, Frances Fitzgerald, was fully aware of the birth register found in the attic of Nurse Doody's former nursing home (St Jude's), yet no investigation has ever been undertaken. The birth register has 1,000 names, some bona fide and some which were illegally registered from 1938 to 1968, including my own name. Why did she never pursue this?

- More recently, in 2013, it was highlighted that Dr Creedon, a GP in Co Monaghan, also arranged illegal adoptions. Why weren't her files and archives scrutinised?

- Why is the Irish government ignoring these illegal practices, thereby contravening Article 7 of the UN Convention on the Rights of the Child, and signed by Ireland in 1990?

I, on behalf of *Adopted Illegally Ireland,* requested the following:

- If an investigation is held into the illegal practices that have taken place since the Adoption Act 1952, would like an investigation of the circumstances of any illegal adoption which is/has been brought to their attention. It requests that garda and/or outside resources be employed if necessary, and all results are made known to the victims of illegal adoption in full accordance with the United Nations Convention on the Rights of the Child.

- The government legislates for files held by the Church to be open so that illegally adopted people can discover their identities. It is known that illegal adoptees' true names are kept at Archbishop's House to ensure adoptees do not marry siblings. The HSE must have the power to open these files, and we request that they be moved to the GRO. We request that files belonging to GPs, nurses and social workers who played a part in illegal adoptions be scrutinised and details be made available to help adoptees find an identity and their family.

- That the government appointed a dedicated team to be more proactive in looking for files that may lie in some former homes' attics, this is in reference to the fact that Nurse Doody's files were recently found in the attic of one of her former nursing homes, namely St Jude's on the Howth Rd. This was the same as the finding of 1,500 files of the Banished Babies. There should be an investigation and a register set up.

- That a contact register is set up for illegal adoptees and run identically to the one available to legally adopted people, the tracing facility needs to be done by date and year of birth within six months either side Currently, no facilities are available that allow birth mothers or their children (illegally adopted) to trace each other.

- That a counselling service is set up for adoptees who have been the victims of illegal adoptions, it's been proven that adoptees, especially those who discovered late in life that they were adopted, suffer from post-traumatic stress but, with proper counselling, can learn to come to terms with it.

I further submitted the following information to undergird our position:

Ireland signed the UN Convention on the Rights of the Child in 1990. Article 7 (Registration, name, nationality, care) declares: All children have the right to a legally registered name officially recognised by the government. Children have the right to nationality (to belong to a country). Children also have the right to know and, as far as possible, to be cared for by their parents. This act continues to be contravened by the Irish State.

Article 8 stipulates that the State should 'respect the right of the child to preserve his or her identity. It also requires that 'where a child is illegally deprived of some or all of the elements of his or her identity, State parties shall provide appropriate assistance and protection, with a view to re-establishing his or her identity speedily.'

It was declared that: ... if the Commission of Investigation is to enjoy the confidence of the adoption community, the Terms of Reference must be as broad as is necessary and reflect the views of those affected most and thus, we call on Minister Reilly to facilitate a debate of the Terms of Reference in the Dáil when it reconvenes in the Autumn. Article 8 of the UN Convention on the Rights of the Child stipulates that the State should 'respect the right of the child to preserve his or her identity, a principle which has been clearly flouted in these instances. Article 8 also requires that '…[w]here a child is illegally deprived of some or all of the elements of his or her identity, States Parties shall provide appropriate assistance and protection, with a view to re-establishing his or her identity speedily.

Findings of the Report

The Commission[10] investigated fourteen mother and baby homes and four county homes between 1922 (when the Irish State was founded) and 1998 (when the last home was closed), detailing the experience of women and children. The investigation covered the causes of infant mortality, burial conditions, forced adoption, and allegations of unethical vaccine trials carried out on residents. The final document was 2,856 pages in length.

When the report was released on 12 January 2021, it revealed stories of appalling conditions, emotional abuse, cruelty, and a high infant mortality rate in institutions run by the State and religious orders from the 1960s onwards.

---

[10] The Terms of Reference specified that only 14 named mother and baby homes were to be included within the scope of the investigation. These are given in the Appendix.

It was reported that:

- Nine thousand children died in the eighteen homes: about fifteen percent of all the children in these institutions.

- There were fifty-six thousand and fifty-seven thousand women in the homes, the greatest number being in the 1960s and early 1970s.

- Before 1960, the lives of 'illegitimate' children in these homes were not saved. In fact, it seemed to be in those homes that reduced their chance of survival.

- The high mortality rates were recorded in official publications and were known to local and national authorities.

The report states:

While mother and baby homes were not unique to Ireland, the number of unmarried Irish mothers admitted was probably the highest in the world—a shockingly high proportion considering how small our island is. However, not all homes were investigated, and it is likely there were a further 25,000 women and children in county homes.

Speaking about the report published on 12 January 2021, Taoiseach Micheal Martin said, 'The regime described in the report wasn't imposed on us by any foreign power. We did this to ourselves as a society. We treated children exceptionally badly. There is no denying society as a collective played a role.

President Michael D Higgins, in response to the commission of inquiry, said,

The publication of the report is not a conclusion but an indication of further work that is required to bring to light a fuller understanding

of what occurred and why, and the need to vindicate the rights of those women and children who resided in the homes.

Reaction to the Report

There was public outrage when the report was released. The measurable facts presented opened the public's eyes and changed people's minds. However, not everyone was happy with either how the investigation had been conducted or the report's contents. Some government officials questioned the legitimacy of the report, claiming that it was biased and incomplete. Others called for an independent investigation to be launched to further explore the issue. The public, meanwhile, demanded that the government act on the findings of the report.

Representative organisations were not given copies of the report before it was released. Survivors '… were invited to a webinar where they were told the government's version, and then they were invited to download three thousand pages.' Catherine Connolly (Leas-Cheann Comhairle) was furious with the government's handling of the release of the report and said, '*Your language and the language of the media told them (the survivors) that they had the report when they didn't have the report.*' Slating the 'three unwise men'—the Taoiseach, Tánaiste and Minister for Children—for not ensuring survivors of mother and baby homes were given copies of the report before it was released to the general public, she stated, *"I am holding this report up to the survivors because they don't have it, not a single survivor has it, and I have had it since yesterday."*

The delivery of the report by Minister Roderick O'Gorman on January 12th, 2021, was a sham. Hundreds of survivors tuned into this webinar meeting without having the report in front of them. I was expecting it to drop on my doorstep any morning before its due date, but alas, no. No physical copies of the report were made available ahead of its online release. How disrespectful to survivors whose testimonies were included in this report. People who opened up to strangers when they had never spoken about what had happened to them before. Independent TD Catherine Connolly voiced her disgust at the way it was delivered, saying 'Members of the Dáil received the executive summary of the report ahead of survivors. They were invited to a webinar where they were told the government's version, and then they were invited to download 3,000 pages', adding, 'Your language, and the language of the media; told them that they had the report when they didn't have the report.'

Of course, not everyone is computer savvy. Many survivors are in their eighties or may not have a computer at home, preventing tens of thousands from joining the webinar. Once again, survivors were ignored. Assuming that there would be an opportunity to answer questions, all who did attend the webinar were on mute. We may as well not have been there.

Catherine Connolly also criticised the report, saying, "Its conclusions ... *bear no connection to the testimonies of the women and men that came forward.*" Despite the renewed trauma incurred in reopening old wounds, many brave women had told their stories. Some had never spoken about their experience. In many cases, their testimonies were watered down or omitted entirely from the report. The harrowing statements in the report showed women being shamed, stigmatised, and punished. Survivors were angry that the investigation found no evidence of sexual abuse. A few cases of physical abuse were reported, but there were many examples of emotional abuse. Survivors were also angry that they were prevented from tracing their family members. Ireland had denied adopted people the legal right to their own information and files, but, at last, the government has promised to change this.

With testimonies ignored and records deleted, the report painted a rosy but inaccurate picture that showed religious institutions in a favourable light. This botched report suits religious institutions perfectly. It allows them to shirk responsibility and avoid putting their hands in their pockets to redress the wrong suffered by thousands of women at their hands. The commission's interpretation did not consider human rights, and its conclusion minimises the survivors' accounts. Did they even listen to the survivors' accounts? Did they not acknowledge how degrading it was for pregnant women to work so hard? How humiliating and degrading it was for the women to pluck grass from the lawns at Bessborough? Many women gave evidence that they were separated from their families for decades and had no idea where they had gone. As a result, laws at the time prevented them from finding them.

The report confirms the stark reality that survivors are side-lined, with academics and historians believing that the testimonies are not worth the printed paper. How could survivor testimonies be excluded when the purpose of the investigation was to investigate the allegations and publish the truth? Perhaps the findings were too disturbing, and Fine Gael, Fianna Fail, and the Church had to be protected at all costs. It is easier to blame society.

Redress for Survivors

Details of the redress scheme were announced on November 16, 2021, by Minister Roderic O'Gorman. He confirmed that up to sixty-five thousand euros (the maximum to a single survivor) would be paid out to survivors of mother and baby homes and county homes. This was deemed unacceptable by survivors as the eight hundred million euros allocated by the State would only benefit thirty-four thousand of the fifty-eight thousand survivors who are still alive. It doesn't take a mathematician to work out that twenty-four thousand would be excluded.

Further, it was announced that only those who had spent more than the first six months of their life in a mother and baby home were entitled to any redress. The reason given for this was that '… babies would not have a memory of their experience.' It seems that the State needs to acquaint itself with some basic knowledge, as 'remembering' the mother is an inadequate criterion. Babies need to be hugged, loved, and fussed over to develop emotionally. Further, as discussed in Chapter 9, being separated from your mother has lasting effects. In fact, thirty professionals working in the area of childhood trauma signed their names to a letter to Roderic O'Gorman asking for the parameters of the mother and baby homes redress scheme to be changed to consider the impact of early trauma. It was stated:

For instance, we know that early separation from a caregiver is intrinsically stressful and has a long-lasting impact throughout the lifespan. Thus, to state that young children who might have been in Mother and Baby Homes for a period of two to three months early in life were less impacted by those who spent longer is simply not scientifically correct. Indeed, the opposite is true. The earlier the impact of trauma, the more long-lasting the effects.[11]

Kathleen Funchion TD, Sinn Fein spokesman, brought a cross-party motion in the Dáil to ensure the redress scheme is changed and survivors' wishes are met. This includes time-based criteria, exclusion of children who had been boarded out, access to an enhanced medical

[11] https://www.thejournal.ie/early-childhood-trauma-mother-and-baby-homes-redress-scheme-5608460-Nov2021/

card scheme, and failure to include some institutions. They are also calling for recourse from religious orders as well as pharmaceutical companies to contribute to the redress scheme. Babies were part of vaccine trials in some of these homes without their mother's knowledge.

The motion took place in the Dáil on 23 November 2021, with many TDs challenging Minister O'Gorman, but despite opposition, the scheme is being implemented. Perhaps the only justification is financial.

However, in justifying his decision, the Minister maintains that the most important thing for children who spent very short periods in institutions is their personal records and birth certificates rather than access to the redress scheme. Delivered through the Birth Information and Tracing Bill, this legislation will provide guaranteed access to un-redacted birth certificates and wider birth and early life information for those who have questions about their origins. Yes, but in addition to redress, are (we) they not entitled to that information anyway? I wonder how Minister O' Gorman concluded that it is more important for survivors to have access to their personal records and birth certificates rather than have access to the redress scheme. Did he ask all 58,000 survivors, or has he just taken it upon himself to make this decision?

There hasn't been one valid reason as to why 'time spent in institutions' has been the deciding factor. Instead, it has been decided that it is in the national interest not to divulge the reason why, as it could upset certain groups of people. Interpreted correctly, 'we're not going to tell you why you have been shafted.' The only reason to base this scheme on time spent in institutions is to save money. There is no other logical explanation. However, if the religious orders were to put their hands deep into their pockets and contribute, everyone would gain, but as always, they are hiding behind a wall of silence while survivors are retraumatised all over again. It is estimated that approximately twenty-four thousand children, now adults, will likely lose out from this tiered scheme, a whopping 40% of survivors.

Independent Review of Illegal Registrations

After the public disclosure of the illegal birth registrations at St Patrick's Guild in Dublin, the government instituted an independent review. Marian Reynolds (former deputy director of social services in Northern Ireland) was appointed to conduct an analysis of other adoption records to determine how widespread the practice may have been. A significant number with suspicious markers were identified in the investigation of a sample of 1,496 files, but illegal birth registrations could not be conclusively identified. However, it was estimated that between five-and-a-half thousand and twenty thousand files in other archives from at least twenty-five adoption agencies could be of illegal adoptions, so a sample of merely one percent is too small for a full investigation. In the St Patrick's Guild case, files relating to incorrect registrations were marked 'as adopted from birth.' A list was established with similar languages, such as 'private adoption' or 'put away, and agencies were asked to comb their files for this type of language or other suspicious markings.

Before her final report was published, Marian Reynolds objected to the names of institutions being redacted and wanted her name to be removed. Her wishes were disregarded, and neither of her requests was agreed upon at a cabinet meeting. Ms. Reynold's report was completed in 2019, but the final report was only published in March 2021. The report's findings were essential as described above: about two hundred and sixty-five files from two agencies had 'suspicious' reference markers, and 'between 5,540 and 19,980 files' may have similar markers.

UN Rapporteur Report

In 2019, following her visit to Ireland in May 2018, the UN Rapporteur, Maude de Boer-Buquicchio, raised serious concerns about the sale and exploitation of children, essentially 'child trafficking, and called for an inquiry into forced and illegal adoptions in Ireland. She highlighted the failure of the State to provide information, accept accountability and offer redress for the survivors of institutional abuse and for individuals adopted in a manner that would amount to the 'sale of children under international law.' Commercial ties to forced and illegal adoptions were also highlighted. She recommended that the inquiry should focus on illegal activity around forced adoptions and requested that rather than focus on individual institutions; the State focus on investigating 'the gamut of human rights abuse' identified in these and similar cases. Ms de Boer-Buquicchio remarked that it was 'widely noted' that many adoption arrangements were made illegally using falsified documentation or by coercing natural mothers to consent to the adoption of their child against their will in both domestic and international settings.

The strong recommendation for a full inquiry into adoption practices based on the compelling evidence presented has so far not yielded much value. The mother and baby homes commission's final report was published in January 2021. Ms de Boer-Buquicchio had previously commented on the terms of the commission: 'Given its limited scope, it could not be comprehensive as it covered only a limited number of institutions. This was also the opinion of many advocates. However, the groundswell of opinion was growing.

Inquiry into Illegal Adoptions

In 2019, high-profile politicians in Ireland called for an investigation into illegal adoptions, and several prominent politicians called on the government to establish an immediate State inquiry into forced and illegal adoptions. Clare Daly, Independent TD (supported by other TDs including Mick Wallace, Joan Collins, Catherine Connolly, Maureen O'Sullivan, Thomas Pringle, and Thomas Broughan), introduced a motion in the Dáil for the State to hold a separate inquiry into adoption practices. Once the illegal registrations at the St Patrick's Guild adoption agency were exposed and it became obvious that the scale of the problem was much larger than previously thought, the then Children's Minister, Catherine Zappone, carried out a scoping exercise on illegal births. The report of the review has never been published. During the session in parliament, Clare Daly remarked that "... *the review itself is limited to looking for evidence of illegal registrations and not illegal adoptions*", adding that "... *the issues around this are much broader than illegal registrations, and they are not presently being examined*".

How Many More Apologies?

Fast forward to 2021, and the conspiracy of silence persists. Findings of illegal adoptions have been excluded from the Commission of Investigation, and there was an abortive plan to seal the records for a period of thirty years for those who had spent time in mother and baby institutions. This was a very hard burden for those who had opened their hearts and souls to the Commission of Investigation. Why? The reason given was that the mothers' privacy needs to be protected; however, data protection is a poor excuse for not advancing the process of restoring people's identities. The commission stated that witnesses were asked to have evidence

142

recorded and that recordings would be later destroyed. However, according to Kathleen Funchion, Sinn Fein TD, and chair of the Oireachtas Committee on Children, some witnesses are adamant that they were not told that the recordings would be destroyed. 'All such recordings were destroyed', according to the commission's report, but there is no written evidence to say that people were told that the tapes would be destroyed.

By a sheer miracle, in February 2022, back-up tapes of the recordings were retrieved. Amazing, when it was thought that they had been totally destroyed. It makes one wonder what other records have been hidden away 'in offsite storage' over the years. Perhaps it was the call to extend the Commission of Investigation beyond 28th February to launch an inquiry into the issue that suddenly someone remembered 'oh yes, there is a backup' Well, I guess the whole survivor community can all breathe a sigh of relief now that we know Minister O' Gorman is the new data controller, and survivor testimonies are safely archived in the Ministers department!

Because most illegal adoptees are unaware of their situation and continue to believe that they are the natural children of their adoptive parents, the true number of illegal adoptions or registrations will never be known. The Adoption Authority of Ireland (AAI) conducted an audit of its files in 2010 and found ninety-nine individuals who had been adopted with no adoption order. In 2014, the acting CEO, Kiernan Gildea, said that it was impossible to indicate the number of illegal registrations. On the National Preference Register, there are a hundred applications for those who are lucky enough to know that they have a birth certificate but were not adopted. He added, 'There must be many thousands in that position who may not even know they are adopted, and their registration is illegal or irregular.'

Court Action

The Commission of Investigation pried wide open a can of worms, the contents of which had been known about by some, suspected by others, and totally unsuspected by many. Once the details of what had taken place in Ireland became public knowledge, there was an understandable demand for those responsible for being held accountable.

However, victims have found it difficult to sue the government without legal or financial backing. The estimated ten thousand euros required before a case even gets to court is beyond the reach of many. Some would like to begin legal action but cannot even start the process due to financial restraints. However, law firms have taken on cases on a pro bono basis, notably those whose illegal registrations were orchestrated by St Patrick's Guild, as revealed in 2018. The initial number of one hundred and twenty-one illegal registrations has now escalated to one hundred and fifty-one, and there are undoubtedly far more.

As my 'adoption' does not fall within the ambit of the State-sanctioned group from St Patrick's Guild, it is more difficult to get assistance from a law firm, despite available evidence. I haven't given up, however, and it is gratifying to know that people in a similar position are suing the Irish State in their individual capacities.

Recently, Derek Linster has commenced legal proceedings against the Irish State, the Minister for Children, and the Attorney General. I admire Derek Linster so much for his tenacity. Derek has been campaigning relentlessly for the Bethany Home and other Protestant institutions to be included in the State's inquiries and redress schemes, for more than twenty years. Bethany Home was one of the eighteen institutions examined as part of the Commission of Investigation into Mother and Baby Homes but was originally not

144

included in the 2002 redress scheme, which was set up under the Residential Institutions Redress Act 2002. This was set up to award persons who had been abused as children while resident in industrial schools. In his autobiography, *Hannah's Shame,* Derek describes how he was born in Bethany Home in Dublin in 1941, the illegitimate child of a Protestant mother and Catholic father living in southern Ireland. The book depicts the poverty he grew up in, to which members of his own Protestant community turned a blind eye, doing little to help him. Deprived of opportunity and brought up without access to any formal education, he subsequently went to England, where he met his wife, Carol, who campaigned with him until her untimely death two years ago. Having met Derek several times, I have been struck by his focus and a strong sense of justice.

In 2014, the Taoiseach announced that the Bethany Home would be included in the investigation. At long last, Derek's campaigning had paid off.

Another case, heard in January 2022, is that of Philomena Lee (eighty-eight years old), whose story was the subject of a book and later an award-winning film, *Philomena,* in 2013. As mentioned previously, Philomena gave birth to her son Anthony in Sean Ross Abbey in Co Tipperary in 1952. He was subsequently taken from her and sent to a couple in America (another of the Banished Babies) without her consent. Despite both parties trying to find each other for decades, they were repeatedly thwarted by the nuns who refused to reveal any information about the other. Sadly, Anthony died without him and his mother ever having a chance to meet. Philomena is among those seeking to have certain findings of the Commission's final report on forced adoptions quashed. She takes issue with the Commission's findings that there was a lack of evidence regarding forced adoptions, citing several discrepancies between her affidavit to the Commission and the content of the Commission's report. I hope

Philomena's case will pave the way for other survivors to take action against the Irish State.

Sadly, Derek Linster passed away on 19th November 2022, aged 81.

A man of integrity and principle. A true warrior R.I.P Derek

Chapter 12
Who is to Blame?

Amazingly, RTÉ, Ireland's national television and radio broadcaster, never followed up media announcements regarding illegal adoptions. In September 2020, I received a message from Isabel Percival, who informed me that RTÉ now had an investigation unit. Sharon Lawless *(Flawless Films)* had investigated this issue for years, but RTÉ had not shown any interest. However, once the report was published and St Patrick's Guild was being investigated for their part in illegal adoptions, revealed in 2018, suddenly RTÉ was interested.

The programme *'Who Am I: Ireland's Illegal Adoptions'* was broadcast in Ireland on 3 March 2020. This publicized, once again, the activities of Dr Eamonn deValera and shone a light on the extent to which some of the country's most elite and powerful individuals acted in contravention of the law. Perhaps they believed they were above the law. A subject that had been ignored and buried for decades was finally exposed to an outraged public. decades was finally exposed to an outraged public.

This documentary was a long time coming, and it has opened the door for further exploration of these illegal adoptions. It has also raised questions about accountability and justice for those affected by these practices. The documentary has hopefully sparked a much-needed conversation about the issue.

What the documentary exposed:

- How religious orders pursued birth mothers for maintenance payments months after their children had been adopted.

- Further documentary evidence of how Professor Eamon de Valera, son of the former president, faked medical appointment documents to facilitate illegal adoptions.

While the issue of illegal adoptions in Ireland is hardly new, many people have only recently learned that they, too, may have been illegally adopted. Emotions are raw. However, the reaction of viewers to the emerging details says a lot about the changing face of Ireland. There has been anger from viewers, with one viewer writing on social media 'How this was allowed to happen, I'll never understand'. Incredibly, this was going on in our midst for decades.

The Church

The power behind these actions was the Church. Whispers about what was going on tend to be dismissed by the public as it was deemed to be beyond reproach. The Church played a prominent role in running our country. It carried great authority with its rigid and strict codes of conduct and clear directives about what was morally acceptable social behaviour. Mary McAleese (a former president of Ireland), in her response to the Commission's report, stated:

The report shows how easy it was to sacrifice women and children to narrow, ludicrous notions of sexual morality. All Christian churches are implicated in the report, but the Catholic Church imposed a culture of fear among uneducated people. It told them emphatically that, through baptism, they were obliged to obey their church's teaching and remain members of that church for life. So, from day one, their right to information was curtailed as well as their freedom of opinion - they had to be obedient to the bishops. [12]

12 The Irish Times, Saturday January 16, 2021

The clergy's greatest condemnation was directed at young unmarried women who fell pregnant. People were reminded to pray for those women who, the congregation was told, would never amount to anything. No decent man would want them. The shame heaped on women in this situation resulted in the perception that society had to get rid of them and they had to be hidden away.

The question must be asked, *who is the sinner? The young, unmarried, pregnant woman, or the abuser of children?* Our mothers were shamed, humiliated, and banished from their parish and family for what crime? They were sometimes sentenced to a life of lonely servitude and heartbreak by having a baby out of wedlock. But it has become apparent that sexual abuse was rife in holy Catholic Ireland and throughout the world and has been allowed to persist for decades. Generally, it was never discussed and swept under the carpet. But it began to be spoken about when victims came forward. In 2002, when *The Boston Globe* investigated allegations of sexual abuse by Catholic priests, abuse by priests was thrust into the national and global spotlight.

In 2018, Pope Francis visited Ireland as part of the World Meeting of Families. It was the first visit from a pontiff since 1979, and the reception was a far cry from Pope John Paul's fanfare forty years before. Yes, things have changed dramatically in Ireland, and its population is much more liberal and secular. With the Church having been rocked by scandals of clerical sexual abuse and the exploitation of women in mother and baby homes, there wasn't the open welcome for the head of the Catholic Church as there had been in previous visits.

However, it is evident that patriarchy is alive and well in the Catholic Church! The pope spent ninety minutes with eight survivors of clerical abuse but denied knowledge of the mother and baby homes or the laundries. This was despite having met Philomena and knowing that her child was kidnapped and trafficked to the U.S.A. The reputation of the priests was important and warranted attention: that of women, less so. That man should not have been allowed step foot on Irish soil.

The then Minister for Children, Catherine Zappone, handed Pope Francis a letter asking for reparation over the Tuam baby scandal. In his reply, the pope made no reference to any financial contribution by the Church but did say he was 'praying that efforts made by both the Catholic Church and the government would help them face responsibility'. A true politician's answer!

Yes, priests, like lay people, are human and make mistakes. However, a lay person would have been punished for the heinous crime of sexual abuse, but instead priests were sent abroad, their abuse of innocent children covered up. The Church enabled the abuse to continue. Pope John Paul II was aware of the abuse during his reign of twenty-six years, starting in 1978—a long time to ignore the abuse of victims. And, of course, there is the seal of the confessional. I guess that a shocking amount of abuse was disclosed by priests and nuns, which the confessional seal protected.

It seems ironic in the extreme that the Church had insurance in place as far back as 1987 to cover liabilities likely to arise from clerical sex abuse. At the beginning of the last century, the Church & General insurance company was formed by the bishops, who still have a nominal share in the company. The Allianz company is now the major shareholder. Between 1987 and 1990, most dioceses were separately insured by Church & General. According to Michael Berni and Pat Neal (who are American experts and part of a leadership team for the 'Protecting God's Children programme to create a safe environment for children and vulnerable adults in the US), globally, the Catholic Church has probably paid out an analogous amount, and '… it is probably reasonable to estimate that the actual "out of pocket" cost of the crisis to the Church internationally is well in excess of two billion dollars. This does not include confidential settlements. The exact amounts may never be known.

The Church is still protected financially, having insurance in place to hedge against financial loss due to abuse claims. We rarely insure for the loss of our children, believing that this would hopefully never happen, and only ensure our assets because it is required. When we insure our property, do we not maintain it to avoid damage and having to claim on our policies? Why did the Church not protect its flock, in the same way, to avoid large pay-outs? More importantly, why did it not ensure that their 'beloved' flock never had their lives destroyed by the people they trusted the most: namely the 'Church'? That obviously was way down on their list of priorities. The Church still blames the secularization of Irish society for the challenges to the faith and rapid change throughout the years, even though the abuse was perpetrated as far back as 1987 and possibly before that.

Nobody seems to be joining the dots. Internationally, horrific events are being uncovered, such as the discovery of 751 children's bodies found under a former residential school in Canada. There are reports of clerical abuse in Chile, Australia, and the United States. There seems to be a pattern with strong links to the Catholic Church: an international paedophile ring that is allowed to continue. There is no sign of remorse from those identified. In fact, in mitigation, the Church's hierarchy argues that such abuse also occurs in other religions and institutions. It seems that this is deemed enough to absolve the Church, but it's just showing the world the extent of the abuse.

Those in the Church may have been insured from the beginning of the 19th century, but they certainly cannot insure themselves against revelations, against people speaking out because they have had enough.

The HSE

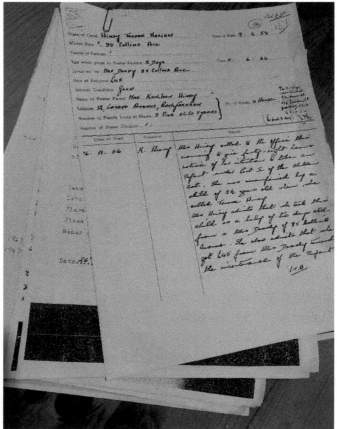

My Life according to the HSE

Throughout this book, the HSE's culpability is exposed. It is apparent that for decades, the HSE, now Tusla, was aware of the widespread falsification of birth records and illegal adoptions throughout Ireland. The practice was given a humane gloss, with those involved claiming it was done to protect the anonymity of the natural mother. However, it was a well-organized baby trafficking scheme allowing couples with enough money to acquire children without vetting. Undoubtedly, highly respected employees of the then Health Board were involved and allowed to practice and become wealthy through the proceeds of 'selling' illegitimate babies. This was despite the Adoption Bill 1952 having come into force. The Adoption Act was amended in 1979, enabling religious orders to shield their assets from their illegal practices of child trafficking and illegal domestic adoptions.

An inspector's report on my file from November 1956 confirms knowledge of my illegal 'adoption,' and I do not doubt that there was a coordinated cover-up effort to protect the professionals involved. I realize the authorities have been aware of illegal adoptions/registrations for years but did nothing.

Identifying people adopted illegally is 'slow work,' was the comment from Tusla. Slow? It took me sixteen years of arduous, heart-breaking searching for my mother, knowing I was racing against time. I was alone in my search, receiving no help or support. I had no idea if she was even alive. And I didn't find my mother in time. I discovered, sadly, that she had passed away in 2009. I suggest that Tusla, which has a fully staffed department, stop making excuses and prioritize the identification of illegal adoptees. Those who have been illegally adopted are owed that much. It is heart-breaking and downright insulting that the fear of the public reaction to the St Patrick's Guild revelation rather than compassion prompted action.

The State

The State is also culpable. In May 2018, Minister Zappone announced that one hundred and twenty-six illegal registrations from St Patrick's Guild had been discovered and that the government would conduct an audit. She further noted that '... until recently, the practice of incorrect registrations has been extremely difficult to prove in most instances because of the deliberate failure of those involved to record any information about it. The implication was that the government had not known about the practice. There are several problems with this announcement. Not only is this number the tip of the iceberg, but the government has known about illegal registrations for years and has ignored requests for audits to be conducted. However, according to the head of the children's charity, Barnardo's, every adoption agency in the country has been involved in illegal registrations, and the file kept on me by the HSE directly contradicts the Minister's statement. The only conclusion that can be reached is that the government has knowingly and systematically ignored revelations of this practice by various advocacy groups over the years.

Further, long after the first legislation regulating adoption in the early 1950s was promulgated, children whose birth mothers would have been in one of forty-two mother-and-baby homes were still being placed with families. Yet, Minister Zappone has claimed that since 1952, all adoptions in which the Irish State was involved were in line with legislation and subsequent legislation. This claim was also made by Charlie Flanagan (TD) on two separate occasions even though an audit, which had been repeatedly called for, had not taken place. The practice can be considered as a crime against the estimated 15,000 (according to Barnardos) infants and their mothers.

Eventually, in 2018, there was an acknowledgment from the government. Speaking in the Dáil, Taoiseach Leo Varadkar noted that there was potentially 'hundreds of thousands of further illegal adoption registration records. He described the practice as 'another dark chapter in our history. It is a crime against children because it robs them of their identity, their heritage, their health histories,' he said, adding, "A lot of women were told after their babies were taken from them that their babies had died and not to enquire about them again." He issued an apology on behalf of the government.[13] This rather underwhelming apology clearly indicates that those of us directly impacted by illegal adoptions are not taken seriously. At the very least, we should have a national apology like that delivered by Julia Gillard, Australia's Prime Minister, in 2013.

I also detect more than a hint of society being blamed by the government. Shame on the Irish government. It is still reluctant to take responsibility. Who is the 'we' the Taoiseach is referring to? Society? No. It is the Church, with State sanction, that is culpable. The State should have monitored the system. There were those who were aware that mothers and their children were suffering abuse, yet the State did nothing. Women were imprisoned. They were subjected to society's discrimination and sanctions and relied on State support. The State had an obligation to protect them, but it failed. It's easier to blame society than to accept responsibility.

Despite *The Irish Examiner* reporter Conall Ó Fátharta consistently writing of the rampant abuse that was part of Ireland's secretive 'adoption' system, the State turned a blind eye, again and again. The reporter's damning words were repeatedly ignored, and the system continued unchecked. It was only when the victims of the system began to speak out that the true extent of the abuse was revealed, and the State was forced to take action.

---

[13] https://www.bbc.Couk/news/world-europe-44305936.

In 2011, the then Minister for Children, Frances Fitzgerald, was asked to launch a statutory inquiry into illegal adoption practices. However, she chose to ignore the request even though she was a trained social worker. She would have had considerable insight into the plight of single mothers and children. Here is an example of another Minister for Children's total lack of empathy. Without a doubt, the disdain with which unmarried women are regarded in Ireland has contributed to the adoption practices in the country.

It is our right to know where we came from, our background, and our medical history. The General Scheme of the Birth Information and Tracing Bill was published in May 2021. The proposed legislation brought by Minister Roderic O' Gorman and Minister Heather Humphries regarding individuals affected by their incorrect registrations was the subject of consultation in the months ahead. The bill covers access to birth and early life information for individuals who were adopted, boarded out, or illegally registered, and hopefully, in time, our birth certificates can be re-registered.

After the discovery of twenty thousand files indicating potential incorrect registrations or illegal adoptions, Minister O'Gorman tasked Prof. Conor O' Mahony, rapporteur for child protection, to investigate the complexities of this situation and recommend a path for any potential future enquiry. Prof. O' Mahony has stated that '... doing nothing is not a credible option for the State in relation to investigating suspected illegal adoptions. He added that the State has a duty to ensure that any potential wrongs are righted and that the process of any potential investigation should be open and transparent. He also suggested that the State should set up a specialised unit to investigate the allegations.

At last, after years of campaigning by other advocacy groups and me, we are finally being listened to. The report, which was released

September 2021, made a series of recommendations for consideration by the government. What is particularly important for those of us who were illegally adopted/registered is how our position will be addressed. With no paper trail, we have had to rely solely on DNA evidence to reconstruct our identity. As I was writing this book before the report submission, I am aware of a time lag before its publication, and it only recently passed through the cabinet. Prof O'Mahoney's report was welcomed and just as anticipated.

The National Archives of Ireland contain just a few snippets, however they are enough to make clear that State officials in 1950s Ireland knew the country was a centre for illegal international baby trafficking. The number of children involved can't even be guessed at, but we can be sure that they were all 'illegitimate.'[14]

The Information and Tracing Bill 2023 was completed on March 9th, 2022, with Minister O'Gorman refusing to accept any of the 300 amendments submitted by opposition TDs. Justifying the Bill, he described it as follows:

...landmark legislation provides guaranteed access in all cases to un-redacted birth certificates and identity information.

- That is not entirely true. An adopted person whose parent has registered a preference for no content will have to attend a mandatory Information session regarding privacy before any birth information, or birth certificate is given to them.

When an information session is required, and a relevant person chooses to abstain, the person can still request a subject access request. That application will then be considered in accordance with the GDPR.

This does not *guarantee access in all cases to un-redacted birth certificates and identity information.'*

The Minister has insisted that some of the amendments were unnecessary because these issues are already covered in the Bill. In addition, certain amendments would restrict the information released (which ones I wonder!). Once again, the Irish State is refusing to listen to us and refusing to listen to their own TDs who submitted the amendments. The Minister is determined to get this Bill passed, another thing out of the way, I'm guessing. How can 300 amendments just be thrown aside? Half of those, perhaps, but not all of them. Just as we all thought that this was a step forward, Minister O'Gorman, although claiming to take our concerns on board, is taking a step backward, showing contempt and disregard for the expertise of all the advocacy groups that have worked so hard.

Finally, one of the changes that were recommended and written into the bill was ...to amend the term 'incorrect birth registration' in the Bill *'to say "falsely or incorrectly recorded'* ...

Activists and advocates, after decades of campaigning, welcomed the recommendation, particularly for parents, relatives of the deceased, people subjected to illegal birth registration, and others affected by the ongoing secrecy of adoption and family separation records.

The Bill permits the adult child of a deceased adopted person or person illegally registered at birth, lawfully boarded/nursed out or institutionalised in a Mother and Baby or County Home institution to apply to TUSLA or the AAI for their parent's information — it only applies if their grandparents (i.e. the parents of their deceased parent) are also deceased (sections 21 to 24).

Counselling and other similar supports will be extended to all affected parties, regardless of contact preferences, including all birth parents, adopted people, and the children of those affected '.

However, there are some adopted people subjected to illegal arrangements who will have no rights under the Bill. Nor does the Bill recognise the rights of people who were in non-adoptive 'care' settings, except for a lawful boarding/nursing out placement or a Mother and Baby or County Home institution. This means that they will have no rights under the Bill and will not be able to access the justice they deserve. The Bill fails to address the rights of those people and the issues they face. This is a major flaw in the legislation that needs to be addressed.

The Final Report – November 2022

In 2017 a Collaborative Forum was formed in order to build upon the process of engagement and consultation with former residents of Mother ad Baby homes. Hosted by the then Minister for Children, Katherine Zappone, the intention was to enable former residents to identify, discuss and prioritise issues of concern. The recommendations of the Forum were published in April 2019; however, its full report could not be published while the matters it referred to were still under consideration by the Commission of Investigation. Eventually, after three years, the report was published in full in November 2022. However, this report that we have waited so long for cannot be considered inclusive.

If the result of an investigation into Mother and Baby homes is to become part of an 'historic analysis,' in the final report, it cannot leave out any group, otherwise, it cannot be regarded as remotely comprehensive and inclusive. Although there has been mounting criticism of the draft law for not offering redress to people who spent less than six months in institutions, The Payment Scheme Bill is continuing through the Irish Parliament. What is not taken into consideration? Not the six months that the government are trying to wriggle out of paying redress but the pain that these women and children lived with for the rest of their lives. No amount of money can make up for that, but to be totally excluded shows a complete lack of empathy and respect from our government.

It says it all as to what Roderic O'Gorman and the state think of us. It infers that the Birth Information and Tracing legislation and the erection of a statute is redress enough. When did any of us agree to any part of this unfair scheme? It is an insult to our intelligence and our sense of justice, and yet another example of the state failing to listen to the voices of survivors and victims of abuse. We have fought for this for years, but now it seems like they are doing us a favour. What arrogance, arrogance that hasn't changed since Irish independence. This is when successive Irish Governments owed a duty of care to their citizens but have been negligent in that duty. Successive Irish Governments, which treated their citizens with contempt, and did not consider them worthy of consideration. Exercising a 'Dominant Position', they abused their powers and failed to put into place laws to protect their citizens, allowing gross miscarriages of justice to take place, by allowing the Catholic Church to take control.

Today in 2023, the government are still showing their contempt by not including those illegally registered/adopted in the redress scheme. But rather offer us a paltry 3.000 euro. An ex-gratia payment they've called it! 3,000 euro for loss of identity and a lifetime of anguish. We were sold; we are owed!

Professor O'Mahoney's Report on Illegal Registrations.

In 2021, following an RTÉ investigation that examined how thousands of Irish babies were illegally adopted over several decades, the Government commissioned a report to be conducted by Prof Conor O'Mahony, the Government's Special Rapporteur on Child Protection, to advise on the next steps. The affected adoptees, all of whom are now adults, were registered at birth as if they were the biological children of their adoptive parents. Minister O'Gorman stated, *"we have known about the practice of incorrect registrations for many years, but it has been extremely difficult to identify and prove in individual cases because of the deliberate failure of those involved to keep records ... This is a very serious and sensitive issue. People have the right to know their true origins and, where we have clear evidence, I believe we are obligated to tell the people affected. Some may know already, but for others, it will be entirely new and very difficult information indeed".*

His statement is quite incorrect. Individual cases that had evidence were never looked at.

The report had 17 recommendations, namely:

- Every person has a legal right to have their identity (including their parentage and their date and place of birth) accurately recorded.

- Despite having knowledge since the early 1950s of the possible existence of a practice of illegal birth registrations and having received an actual admission of the practice as early as 1992, the State failed until 2010 at the earliest to take sufficient steps to prevent the practice; to investigate its scale, or to remedy its effects. It is incumbent on the State to take all practicable measures to remedy these violations without further delay.

- It is a matter for persons affected by the practice of illegal birth registrations to indicate whether they wish to receive a State apology.
- The proposals contained in the Birth Information and Tracing Bill regarding a Register of Acknowledged Identity, which would allow a person affected by illegal birth registration to have the details of the registration of their birth corrected while also continuing to legally use the identity which they have used all their life, are endorsed as striking the correct balance.
- Adoption tracing legislation providing unqualified access to birth certificates, adoption files and other early life information, both for formally completed adoptions and for incomplete adoptions resulting in illegal birth registration, should be enacted at the earliest possible opportunity.
- Adoption records currently in private hands should be acquired by the State and held in a centralized archive.
- To avoid further lengthy delays in delivering a remedy to individuals affected, a targeted and focused approach should be adopted that builds on the Independent Reviewer's report.
- A Specialist Tracing Team should be established and provided with ring-fenced resources to ensure that it does not negatively impact other adoption tracing work.
- The Specialist Tracing Team should conduct a full trace on files flagged by Tusla as suspicious during the independent review process to establish which (if any) of these cases can be confirmed as cases of illegal birth registration and identify the potential for further targeted investigation of other adoption files.

- If necessary, the Birth Information and Tracing Bill should provide legal authority for the work of the Specialist Tracing Team, as well as any similar future activity by either Tusla or the Adoption Authority of Ireland aimed at investigating historical irregularities in adoption practices.

- There should be a right to request the Specialist Tracing Team to conduct an expedited review of cases involving a reasonable suspicion of illegal birth registration. This right should extend to the person potentially affected and their children. Such reviews should involve the use of both documentary and DNA evidence.

- The Birth Information and Tracing Bill, in its enacted form, should ensure that DNA evidence can play a full part both in tracing and in the provisions governing the correction of the register and adopt an approach that is not unduly prescriptive in respect of what forms of DNA evidence or information from genealogical databases will be accepted.

- The Status of Children Act 1987 should be amended to allow for mandatory DNA testing of relatives other than potential parents in appropriate cases, with suitable safeguards included to ensure this power is used proportionately.

- Provision should be made to cover the legal costs of persons affected by illegal birth registrations. Such provision should be sufficient to ensure that individuals who need to apply for a declaration of parentage (including potential DNA testing) should be able to make an application without undue delay.

- A State inquiry into illegal adoptions (broadly defined) should be established on a non-statutory basis. The inquiry should adopt the truth commission model and be informed by principles of transitional justice. The inquiry's scope, composition, and working methods should be determined in consultation with persons affected by illegal adoptions, and consideration should be given to including such a person as a full member of the inquiry.

The report included a final recommendation that the report "be published in full and at the earliest available date" and that "an advance copy be provided to persons affected by illegal birth registration that are known through previous engagements either with the Department of Children, Equality, Disability, Integration, and Youth or with the Special Rapporteur.". The Special Rapporteur noted that this recommendation *"is aimed at learning from dissatisfaction expressed by affected persons in relation to the manner in which past reports on historical issues have been published."*

Recommended also to the extent that he can arrange for contact with affected individuals, the Minister will host an online briefing on the report and the Government response. He will ensure that a copy of the report is provided to them in advance of publication. He will also ensure that hard copies are made available to anyone who prefers this format to electronic soft copies.

To this day (1st March 2023), I have not received a copy of the report due before the online briefing. The online briefing consistently referred to Illegal adoptions/registrations and a one-off sum of 3,000 euros to be paid to those affected individuals whose illegal adoptions were facilitated by St Patricks Guild, representing a contribution towards DNA testing and legal fees.

And what about the rest of us? The report was to include all illegal registrations, and nowhere does it mention 'only St. Patricks Guild. Perhaps as an afterthought this is now to include individuals who were illegally registered as part of a private arrangement as well as those who were boarded out. The Government has also said that it would offer those affected an apology in Dáil Eireann during the advancement of the upcoming Birth Information and Tracing Bill. *Talk is cheap; I think that more than an apology is needed.*

The Professionals

It was not just those at St Patrick's Guild who were involved. As mentioned previously, Mrs Keating ran an illegal adoption racket from her private nursing home, St Rita's, in Ranelagh. She falsely registered babies as the natural children of the couples who acquired them from their mothers. Although St Rita's was investigated in 1954, and there were potential imprisonable offences committed by all those involved, there were no prosecutions.

Further, gynaecologists, social workers, GPs, and priests with connections to these homes, some of whose names were known to the authorities, all played a part. The authorities were very aware of how prevalent the practice was. There is anecdotal evidence that Charles Haughey, the Taoiseach at the time, had said that TDs had fathered half the children born in St Rita's!. No wonder Mrs Keating was allowed to continue; she had the protection of influential people. After the Keating investigation, the authorities had information about the names and addresses of all the Irish birth mothers whose children were illegally taken from St Rita's.

A letter published in *The Irish Mail on Sunday,* 1 February 2015, showed that Eamon de Valera, professor of gynaecology at University College, had been involved in the illegal adoption of babies in the 1960s and the issuing of a birth certificate in the name of the adoptive parents, exactly as had happened in my case. The letter, addressed to the doctor of an 'adopted' man and signed by de Valera, was in response to an inquiry from the adoptive parents about their 'adopted' child's medical background. It stated:

I am aware of the boy you have noted in your letter. I can confirm no adoption certificate was necessary at the time because there was no further communication between the boy and his biological mother. An arrangement was made in the late 60s for his new family. Given his illegitimate background, we felt it best that the child was placed with a good family as a matter of urgency.

Children were considered to be commodities, fulfilling a parent's longing to have a family while lining the pockets of those involved.

Over several decades, de Valera arranged for babies born to unmarried mothers to be 'adopted' by couples who could not conceive children. In one case, deValera is accused of facilitating the 'adoption' of four children by one family over five-and-a-half years.

. None of these now adults were aware that they had been adopted, let alone illegally adopted. To facilitate an illegal adoption, de Valera arranged what was known as fake pregnancies. Regular 'antenatal' appointments for women who were not pregnant were made. On the date the identified baby was due to be born, the woman would enter the designated hospital and leave with 'her' (illegally adopted) baby.

Until the 1970s, Dr Irene Creedon, a GP from county Monaghan, arranged dozens of illicit and illegal adoptions across Ireland over a period of two decades. She took babies from vulnerable mothers, giving their place of birth as her surgery and then allowed adoptive parents to register these babies as their own biological children. The practice came to light when Margaret Norton, who was aware that she had been 'adopted,' tried to trace her birth mother. She discovered that she had been handed over as a baby to her adoptive parents in a hotel car park in Co Louth and (following the same pattern as other illegally adopted babies) was registered as their own. Her place of birth was given as Dr Creedon's surgery. Margaret was not the only one; it emerged that was a string of others who were also registered as being born at the surgery. Astonishingly, the Adoption Board and its successor, The Adoption Authority, were informed of Dr Creedon's activities as far back as 2005. Even more astonishing is the statement made by Dr. Creedon's daughter implying that her mother was a heroine:

She helped a lot of people. They were from different times and different eras. People came to her when they needed help, whether to give up a child or adopt a child. My mother was a wonderful person, a heroine. She was an extraordinary woman.

This 'heroine' knowingly broke the law in the Adoption Act (1952) by allowing couples to falsely register babies right up to the 1970s, leaving several people without an identity and who have no way of discovering who their birth parents are.

Another culpable person is Nurse Doody. As mentioned previously, her birth registry recorded a thousand births (some of them married women) from 1938 until 1968. The only way many other illegally registered people and I could be identified in the register, was from our date of birth. This made it virtually impossible for our birth mothers to find us or for us to find our birth mothers.

Society

But it takes two to produce a baby. Where are all the men who were responsible for fathering a child and, in some cases, abusing women's and girls' bodies? Why weren't these men made to pay? Those who did fight for their children found themselves up against the village gossip and the eagle eye of the parish priest. Of course,

Catholic-led Irish society liked to take the moral high ground, looking down on the weak and vulnerable from a very male high horse. Who made these rules? Of course, men did. And Ireland was transformed into a patriarchal society that lasted for decades. Women were denied a voice and their rights. They were relegated to the lower rungs of society, and women who had babies out of wedlock filled the very lowest rung.

So, while looking back, it is easy to see how the actors (the Church and State) were able to influence and rule the population with an iron fist, without any empathy for women such as Terri and, indeed, my mother and thousands like her. Some could perhaps argue that it was accepted during those times, but surely cruelty is not acceptable in any era. It is essential to value the individual, no matter what the context, and to respect their right to make their own decisions. We must also strive to create a fairer and more equitable society, where all people are treated with dignity and respect.

The Redress Scheme

As I write my book the final vote of the Mother and Baby redress scheme was passed at report stage on 22nd February 2023 and will now go to the Seanad. The scheme, debated in the Dáil for over four hours totally rejected the amendments put forward by the opposition. An overwhelming 73 against, and 62 for, leaving 24,000 survivors excluded from the scheme. Minister O'Gorman offered no reasonable justification for such an arbitrary policy. Instead, he has tried to divert attention from the scheme by promoting the new birth information and tracing legislation, a right that we are all entitled too.

A done deal before it started. It's a sad day for all of us, once again leaving us discriminated against and all because of the six-month rule that states you must have spent six full months in an institution as a child. One day less, and that is where exclusion begins, adding to the suffering of those who have already suffered. Nor does it cater for people who were boarded out as children, (the forerunner to fostering); people subjected to vaccine trials, racism, or other discrimination and of course the government's 'Achilles' heel'; illegal adoptees. Although members of the public have repeatedly called for the scheme to be extended through an email campaign and despite knowing what the Irish people want, the government completely disregarded their demands.

The anguish on the faces of the TDs who supported us was palpably visible and I thank all of those who supported us. Holly Cairns[15], the Social Democratic TD said:

"The denial of justice and disregard for survivors is startling. The minister is directly responsible for crafting and leading this process, but every Government backbencher and independents who quietly vote with them share culpability for this injustice."

Richard Boyd-Barrett[16]. (People before Profit TD), himself born in a Mother and Baby home said *"the redress scheme should finally give people who passed through the mother and baby home system, the closure and the justice that they deserve but that's not happening"*.

I feel sorrow for our mothers and children who have passed; still in death discriminated against; mothers and now adult children who are still searching, part of the 34,000 excluded. Have they not suffered enough? Surely it should make no difference whether you were just

---

[15] Journal.ie
[16] Journal.ie

one day, one week or six months in an institution. The primal wound has begun once the mother and child are separated.

Decades later people are still suffering, all due to the States failure to make things better. Now is their chance to make amends for all the wrongs they and the church have inflicted on vulnerable mothers and their children. Instead, Minister Roderic O'Gorman fails to recognise the consequences of forced family separation as well as lack of identity. Leo Varadkar's[17] (Taoiseach) statement that the 800 million euros that will be given as redress to the 34,000, *"could otherwise be spent meeting the needs of today and trying to build a better future"*, sums up how the State views us. However, the Church has never been approached to dig deep into their long pockets to contribute to this redress scheme. That same Church who profited from covertly selling babies to Irish or US Catholics for adoption benefited by up to $50 million in today's money.[18]

This deeply flawed, shameful redress scheme will continue to haunt and be revisited repeatedly in the future. This important issue is not resolved. It will reopen like a festering wound that has not been treated and in history books in years to come, it will show how, once again, survivors were oppressed and denied their rights and deserved nothing. There is no real redress, nor any form of humanity within their Bill.

---

[17] Prime Minister of Ireland
[18] Banished Babies by Mike Milotte

Eamon de Valera's son was involved in unlawful adoption of 'illegitimates'

Proof that nation's top gynaecologist bypassed the courts to give baby to new family 'as a matter of urgency'

By Alison O'Reilly

FAMILY: Eamonn de Valera Jr, right with his father and brother Ruairc

PROFESSOR EAMONN DE VALERA
MR MAO, FRCPI, FRCOG, FICS

THE son of former taoiseach Eamon de Valera was involved in illegal adoptions in the 1960s.

Professor Eamonn de Valera Jr, who was a consultant gynaecologist at Holles Street, bypassed the courts to arrange for the children of unmarried mothers to be adopted by couples families.

A document seen by the Irish Mail on Sunday reveals how the high-ranking doctor arranged for a baby boy to be illegally adopted in the 1960s by facilitating his adoptive parents to sign his birth cert.

Last night the Adoption Authority of Ireland said it was shocked and appalled by the revelation and called for an immediate Garda investigation and for this evidence to be included in the nuclear and baby home inquiry.

The adopted man at the centre of the controversy was born at the National Maternity Hospital to Holles Street. In the letter, dated July 17,

'We felt it best the child was placed with a good family'

1985, the late professor, responding to a query by the adoptive family of the child about his medical history, said: 'I am aware of the boy you have asked in your letter. I can confirm no adoption certificate was necessary at the time because there was to be no further communication between the boy and his biological mother.

'No arrangements was made for a birth certificate in the late 1960s for his new family. Given his illegitimate background we felt it best the child was placed with a good family as a matter of urgency.'

The letter, signed by de Valera, was sent to the family doctor of the adopted man. The man, who is now in his 60s and does not wish to be identified, told the MoS he had no desire to find his birth mother but needed his medical records.

'I always knew I was adopted. My family were never anything but honest with me about it,' he revealed, was of little importance. They couldn't have a child so the couple help from Dev. He was clearly in a position where he had access to children of unmarried mothers and could arrange for them

to be sent to a family like mine.

'My parents always said I was adopted. They never lied, but the mention of my birth certificate came up and my mother simply said, "But you've none. That's how I will always be."

'It was only when I got into my seventies that I suffered chest difficulties and I showed a lot of breath, urgently went to hospital and I had no trace of any of my arteries.

'We had no medical history. The point of call was Dev. Our family doctor because involved and he

wrote directly to Dev and he responded. He clearly had no information about my biological family because, well, she had me. She gave me up and she was gone.

'How could the baby who had no idea where to find me? There are no records, so it's for this reason I want to open the door to her. While I'm never asking for her, I want her to know I'm here.'

The Adoption Act was introduced in 1952. After that, any adoption without a court order was illegal.

An estimated 1,500 children were illegally adopted and placed with families both here and abroad.

'The agency was clearly bypassed deliberately'

Speaking to the MoS last night, chief executive Patricia Carey said the Adoption Authority of Ireland

was 'shocked and appalled.'

'There was a State agency set up to conduct adoptions and it was clearly by-passed deliberately.

'That element of Prof de Valera's activities should be included in the mother and baby home commission. The records of the hospital should be scrutinised to ensure we know if there were other illegal adoptions.'

De Valera, who skittered singer

Sinéad O'Connor, was not the only person involved in illegal adoptions. The MoS previously uncovered 19 such adoptions facilitated by Dr Charles Creedon over a 20-year period.

In a statement, the General Registry Office said: 'There has been an investigation of illegal adoptions by the GRO. The only aware of two such cases which took place before the Adoption Act 1952 came into effect.'

alison.oreilly@mailonsunday.ie

COMMENT Page 8

The dazzling career of an aristocrat of Irish medicine

By Alison O'Reilly

EAMONN de Valera was born on October 11, 1913, the second son and third child of Eamon and Sinéad Seán de Valera. His mother Sara O'Doherty in April 1941.

He was educated at Blackrock College, Dublin and graduated from University College Dublin in 1936 as a bachelor of medicine going on to become one of the leading maternity professionals of his era, working at the National Maternity Hospital, Holles Street, and professor of obstetrics and gynaecology in UCD in 1960. He was invested as a Fellow of the Royal College of Obstetricians and Gynaecologists in 1970.

Dr de Valera was named in a submission by the Survivors of Symphysiotomy group in a submission to the UN Committee Against Torture as one of the doctors who carried out the practice of breaking a women's pelvis as an alternative to a Caesarean section. One woman said he had carried out the procedure on her in 1957.

He was a pro-life amendment advocate. He died in 1996, four years after the letter confirming the irregular adoption was sent from his Shrewsbury Road home.

PROOF:
The 1985 letter signed by Prof de Valera to the GP of a man who was adopted in the 196...

EPILOGUE

At long last, Irelands people are no longer hoodwinked. The only way the treatment of young, unmarried women was allowed to persist over decades was because high-ranking politicians and judiciary officials were either complicit or turned a blind eye. Some may still be alive. Yes, State sanctions on a massive scale in holy Catholic Ireland. Why is the Church still allowed to run our schools and manage our national maternity hospitals? Despite the cruelty shown, why does the Catholic Church continue to have access to mothers and children?

Truth speaks volumes, and I am sure those culpable never thought so many thousands would one day speak out about what happened. It is indeed a sign of how times have changed and how popular culture and various advocacy groups helped embolden victims to come forward and offer them support. There is still a long way to go in terms of cultural and systemic changes, but the initial steps are being taken and the message is clear - no one should have to suffer in silence. Thanks to victims' groups, the public became aware of how mothers and babies were treated. The wall of silence, at last, has been broken.

Since I first registered on a DNA database, the number of people in DNA databases has increased from about eight million to about twelve million, so the 2017 figures are already out of date. As more people register, the percentage of successful traces will increase exponentially. It is going to become easier and easier for adoptees to find their birth families. This was the key commentary message on the 2016 Adoption Bill submitted by members of the ISOGG Ireland group in June 2018 to the Irish government. [19]

[19] Genetic Genealogy Ireland: ISOGG Ireland commentary on the proposed Adoption Bill 2016. Monday 5 March 2018:

I subsequently met with representatives of the Department of Child and Youth Affairs and impressed upon them the increasingly important role DNA will play in helping adoptees trace their birth families. Ireland has experienced many inter-country adoptions over the last decade or so (with countries such as Russia, China, Africa and others). As these children grow up, many will want to know their ethnic makeup and where they come from, which their DNA can show. They may even want to use DNA to reconnect with birth family members in these various countries. Indeed, the use of DNA has resulted in successful outcomes in cases of childhood abduction. A man in China was reunited with his parents after being abducted as a two-year-old toddler thirty-two years ago. The joy on his mother's face when they reconnected was indescribable as she had searched for him for decades, never giving up hope. I have helped quite a few adoptees use DNA in this way. And over the past year, many have been referred to me by adoption agencies within Ireland, indicating that social workers appreciate the importance of this new technology for their work.

For the mothers, too, there is hope where there was none before. There is more and more interest among the mothers who gave their children up for 'adoption,' many of whom are now in their 70s and 80s. Even if their child does not immediately appear in their DNA match list, their results will always be available. If their child joins the database many years after they have passed on, their presence in the database will send the message that they had taken the trouble to search for the child they had had to give up. This can be a great source of comfort for many adoptees.

https://ggi2013.blogspot.com/2018/03/isogg-ireland-commentary-on-proposed.html

It should be emphasized that DNA is only one part of the equation. Genealogy is the other part, and the two-go hand in hand. If there is no instant match to the immediate family, some standard genealogical work will be necessary. This may take months or even years. In 2017, the average length of time needed to find a birth parent was about two years. But this time frame will decrease as the numbers increase in the database. Recently, I traced the African family of an Irish mixed-race adoptee. In a few years, this will be commonplace. It is simply a waiting game, as described by Maurice Gleeson earlier.

A future where DNA results would be easily accessible was previously unimaginable. Thanks to our wonderful scientists, we have discovered the identity of our biological families. Future generations (given the combination of DNA testing and the internet) may be unable to comprehend how identities were ever kept secret.

Even more important is how we can learn about our family's medical history. The secret that was kept from me for forty-eight years had dangerous effects. All my life, I had been giving incorrect medical histories to doctors. Any potential genetic illnesses that may have been passed down were unknown to me and, therefore, not preventable. It is staggering to think of the possible consequences for my children from not knowing my medical background and me. Luckily, I have always enjoyed perfect health, so I assume my birth mother and father had good genes.

I waited in anticipation and with the hope that Prof. O' Mahony's report would present a positive conclusion regarding illegal adoptions, particularly illegal registrations. Mothers who were forced to give up their babies hope that one day they will be reunited with their child; illegal adoptees or those of us who were wrongly registered hope that we will discover our identity and develop a clear sense of who we are. Although the lost years can never be replaced,

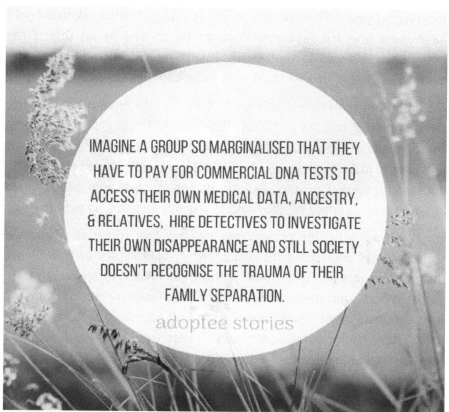

IMAGINE A GROUP SO MARGINALISED THAT THEY HAVE TO PAY FOR COMMERCIAL DNA TESTS TO ACCESS THEIR OWN MEDICAL DATA, ANCESTRY, & RELATIVES, HIRE DETECTIVES TO INVESTIGATE THEIR OWN DISAPPEARANCE AND STILL SOCIETY DOESN'T RECOGNISE THE TRAUMA OF THEIR FAMILY SEPARATION.

adoptee stories

finding closure is important for us. We will be able to make sense of our own behaviour and that of others. We will be able to understand why our mothers and we endured our profound losses and, in some way, find a resolution to our pain. Ultimately, we will be able to find peace and healing because we now know the truth.

Importantly, the government may finally draw a line under this part of our history and admit responsibility. To do otherwise will ensure that the matter drags on for years. It is likely that I will never be able to put what happened fully behind me. That is despite having achieved what I set out to do. It has been 21 years since I discovered I wasn't who I thought I was, but my poor mother lived with her secret for over 50 years. Her life was probably one of heartbreak that could have been avoided. There will never be an end to all this if the government refuses to thoroughly investigate illegal adoptions and acknowledge that this went on with their knowledge.

Although the Professors report was casually brushed aside with, the mention of redress to 126 St Patricks Guild illegal registrations, by Minister O'Gorman. Nowhere in the report did Professor O'Mahony mention St Patrick's Guild. His remit included all illegally adopted/registered people. Definitely not on the same page! Once again, we are ignored by the State as though it never happened.

If it wasn't for the perseverance of amateur historian Catherine Corless, who uncovered the Tuam baby scandal in 2014, with her outstanding report, there would never have been an investigation by the Irish State into mother and baby homes. Changes would not have taken place. People would never have had access to what is rightly theirs, their background information. Years would have elapsed, and people would have lived and died with the anguish of what happened to them. For illegally adopted/registered people like me, however, we are still side-lined. What about the suspicious files identified during an independent review process in 2019? Prof. O'Mahony's call for an investigation into illegal registrations has been ignored, akin to Marion Reynolds objection to the redaction of some of the institutions in the Commission of Investigation, along with her request not to include her name in the report. Her wishes were disregarded at a cabinet meeting, and neither of her requests was agreed upon. Mr O'Gorman said that the upcoming Birth Information and Tracing Bill 2022 *"robustly fulfils the vast majority of the recommendations".* That's not good enough it doesn't cover everything for all of us, but for him, the progression of the bill was more important, a 'priority' for him as minister (his words). In the end, nothing has changed.

Ultimately, these numerous public scandals indicate how people have become dehumanized in the eyes of officialdom. People's feelings were deemed not to matter. It seems certain that these terrible things were allowed to happen due to the failure of the State to treat its citizens equally. This may change in time when everyone matters; perhaps then further atrocities will be avoided.

Least we never forget Ireland's holocaust, where women and babies were worked to death and buried in mass graves. Where babies were taken and sold like cattle!

I Cry a Tear for Ireland.

I cry a tear for Ireland, my heart sad at you.

Its place in history remembered for things as human brutality upon human do.

I cry a tear for Ireland, my head bowed in shame

For You will be remembered, for Your misery and pain,

that you cause time and time again.

I cry a tear for Ireland will you ever learn?

The sadness the heartbreak that you inflict. It now needs to end,

Let the word be spread.

Seamus Sharkey Kelly.

APPENDIX

Plans for 'Adoption' of Theresa:
Kathleen Hiney's Account

I was young and naïve. I had my daughter Margaret who was five, and I did not want her to be an only child, so I really wanted another, and it did not seem like biologically I would be able to conceive another.

One day my husband met a friend of his, Jack Mahon, now deceased. He lived at Haddington Place; his little girl was around seven or eight at this time (1952). He told him he and his wife had been lucky enough to adopt a little girl of about six or seven years old. He told my husband he might be able to put him in contact with someone (I don't know who exactly, it could have been Miss Hannon) who could help us. We then heard no more for a few months.

Suddenly one Friday, there was a knock on the door around 1954, and a very nicely dressed woman introduced herself as Ms. Hannan. I invited her in (as you would have done to well-to-do-looking people at the time). She said she understood I was looking to adopt a baby. She told me her daughter Mareece was the almoner at the Coombe Hospital, and she knew of a girl who was expecting a baby and would not be able to bring her home. She never said what she did. She also didn't mention much about Theresa's mother.

I was over the moon and agreed immediately. Ms. Hannan brought me in her car with her driver to meet Dr. Keane. I can't really remember where... Northumberland Road springs to mind, but I could not be sure. He asked me if I would accept the baby even if it were handicapped, and I said yes. They said it was very gallant of me. They said they would update me on the pregnancy. I used a public phone to call him (I think it was his home ... almost certain. Unless it was somehow attached to the Coombe Hospital) all the time, looking for updates. I was so excited.

I received a telegram (I don't have this anymore) from Dr Keane to tell me the baby had been born. He told me she had lovely ears. When she was three days old, my husband and I went with Mrs. Hannan to collect the baby (Collins Avenue). We went to her (Nurse Doody's) house, and there was nothing to suggest there was a baby there; it was sparsely furnished. A young boy, it must have been Nurse Doody's son, answered the door and let us in. He said to Nurse Doody, 'Mam, you'll have to stop doing this. Theresa was on the ground in an orange box wrapped in cotton wool on the floor. I was not told about Theresa's background or her name. Nurse Doody told me the mother's name was Brigid. I did not know anything else.

As I had no money, Nurse Doody had asked Dr. Keane if he could cover the price of the pram and the baby clothes, which he did. I'm not sure when I asked for this, but I think it was before I took Theresa.

Nurse Doody said to use the side door to leave; I presumed that Brigid was in the house, and this must have been so that Theresa's mother would not see us. This was implied — I presumed it would be traumatic for the mother. I didn't see Brigid.

I think I first met Nurse Doody at Dr Keane's house (again, I can't remember where ... possibly Northumberland Road). I do not really know who instigated the 'adoption'—Nurse Doody or Mrs. Hannon. Nurse Doody did pay me £45 in one lump sum. I do not know where she got this from. Nurse Doody came to the christening at Donnycarney Church. I had a friend as a godparent. The baby was present.

There did not seem to be any legal process; I did not sign or was not informed about anything and didn't ask.

I registered my birth in Cabra West, where I lived. They didn't ask anything. I just said she was born at home. Mrs. Hannon had said to 'do it legally. This went over my head. I'm not really sure what she meant. At some stage, she had told me this in the car, her chauffeured car. It could have been after we picked up Theresa. I had registered Margaret before. I knew you had to register a baby. No one told me to do this.

In 1956 there was a crisis in Hungary, and the Red Cross was appealing to people to adopt babies, so I said we would again. We heard about a place in Rathfarnham where we could inquire about this. I rang about it and found out information but never actually went there.

Then in 1956, I had another visit from Mrs. Hannan. I was pleased to see her. She asked if I knew anyone who was anxious to take a baby girl. She was two weeks old with gastroenteritis at St Ultan's hospital.

We decided to adopt this baby, who is now my daughter Bernadette. Mrs. Hannon arranged for us to visit St Kevin's Health Board. I brought Theresa, who was now two years old. St Kevin's is now St James's Hospital. I went by myself, and we met Mrs. Neary of the Health Board.

Mrs. Neary of the Health Board interviewed me. She asked me about Theresa. She asked if she was my own. I said yes, and her attitude completely changed. She said she knew 'all about' Theresa. I became highly distressed and started crying. Mrs. Neary was extremely rude and told me to sit. She told me she'd be out at my home at three o'clock. She presented me with two forms, one for Theresa and one for Bernadette and told me to sign them, which I did. I must have been backdating and regularising Theresa's adoption. I didn't read them. I was so upset. She never asked me about Mrs. Hannan; I could not remember if she did.

Bernadette was fostered out to me. I was only supposed to have her for weekends in the beginning, but after one particular weekend, I never gave her back. After about three months, I got a letter from the Health Board asking me to bring her in. I feared I might go to prison, but they said nothing and were delighted the baby was healthy and receiving individual attention. I never had further issues regarding my guardianship of Bernadette after that.

Mrs. Neary visited once a month and was always aggressive. She surveyed the house. My husband eventually told me not to let her in. She threatened me with the police, so I had to. I became so upset by her visits I told her she could take Theresa. This was a bluff, and she never did. After Mrs. Neary, two more case workers would visit – Ms. McCarthy, who was nice, and a younger girl, who was also nice.

My finances were extremely strained at times. I asked Mrs. Neary for clothes, but she said they were not obliged to provide the children with anything. The method of 'adoption' I'd signed for—private adoption with the hospital, I think, rather than doing it the correct way with the Health Board on Navan Rd, where you only gave the Health Board 24 hours' notice, and which only obliged the Health Board to essentially make sure the children were alive but no more than that. She gave me nothing. She would not help me even though we were extremely poor.

Years later, the Health Board claimed they could not track Nurse Doody or Dr Keane. They are covering it all up. We found them on the internet. Dr Keane was still practicing years later. I believe Nurse Doody was known to the Health Board, that she was known for organizing these 'adoptions.' Mrs. Nearly became so angry. She had found out about Theresa. I think Mrs. Hannon might have told Mrs. Neary about Nurse Doody, but I cannot be sure. I told Theresa everything, but I cannot be sure when.

Bernadette was fostered and never officially adopted.

Private Homes that facilitated illegal adoptions/registrations not investigated by the Commission of Investigation

- St Judes, Howth Road, Raheny, Co Dublin, facilitated by Nurse Doody
- St Rita's, Ranelagh, Co. Dublin facilitated by Mrs Marie Keating
- Mrs Norman, Marie Clinic. Howth Rd, Clontarf. Co. Dublin
- Dr Creedon, Co. Monaghan arranged private adoptions not from her home.

Homes Investigated by The Commission of Enquiry

- Ard Mhuire, Dunboyne, Co Meath.
- Belmont (Flatlets), Belmont Ave, Dublin 4.
- Bessboro House, Blackrock, Cork.
- Bethany Home, originally Blackhall Place, Dublin 7 and from 1934, Orwell Road, Rathgar, Dublin 6.
- Bon Secours Mother and Baby Home, Tuam, Co Galway.
- Denny House, Eglinton Rd, Dublin 4, originally Magdalen Home, 8 Lower Leeson St, Dublin 2.
- Kilrush, Cooraclare Rd, Co Clare.
- Manor House, Castlepollard, Co Westmeath.
- Ms. Carr's (Flatlets), 16 Northbrook Rd, Dublin 6.
- Regina Coeli Hostel, North Brunswick Street, Dublin 7.
- Sean Ross Abbey, Roscrea, Co Tipperary.
- St. Gerard's, originally 39, Mountjoy Square, Dublin 1.

- <u>St Patrick's Mother and Baby Home</u>, Navan Road, Dublin 7, originally known as Pelletstown, and subsequently transferred to Eglinton House, Eglinton Rd, Dublin 4; and

- The Castle, Newtowncunningham, Co Donegal.

In addition, a 'representative sample' of state-operated county homes, selected by the Commission as fulfilling a function similar to the mother and baby homes, were included. These are:

- St Kevin's Institution (Dublin Union)

- Stranorlar County Home, Co Donegal (St Joseph's)

- Cork City County Home (St Finbarr's)

- Thomastown County Home, Co Kilkenny (St Columba's)

Several homes, such as Bessborough House (Cork), Bon Secours (Galway), Manor House (Westmeath), Sean Ross Abbey (Tipperary) and St Patrick's (Dublin), had been identified as sources for illegal domestic and foreign adoptions. Many of the children in these homes were trafficked to the U.S.A.

References:

- Banished Babies: The Secret Story of Ireland's Baby Export Business by Mike Milotte

- The Lost Child of Philomena Lee: The Heart-breaking Story of a Mother and her fifty year search for her son by Martin Sixsmith

- Women who run with the Wolves by Clarissa Pinkola Estes

- The Primal Wound by Nancy Verrier

- The Light InThe Window. A moving account of the cruel reality of life inside a home for unmarried mothers in 1950s Catholic Ireland by June Goulding

- 'Adoption Stories'-Sharon Lawless/Flawless Films

Timeline 1973-One Family Ireland -unmarried-mothers-allowance.

The Contraceptive Bill of 1985-Irish News Archives.

Andrew Martin-19/02/2015

P.M. Garrett, "The Hidden History of the PFIs: The Repatriation of unmarried mothers and their children from England to Ireland in the 1950s and 1960s.

Nearly 9,000 children died in 'brutally misogynistic' homes for unmarried mums

Metro News.co.uk-12/01/2021-*Tom Williams*- 2nd Chance Adoption-Wasatch International Adoption (wiaa.org)

National Apology Forced Adoptions gov.au-

The Grief Recovery Method-2017/grief adopted children.

Scientists discover children's cells living in mothers' brain.

Scientific American-*Robert Martone*. 04/12/2012

What is Kafala – Kafala.org/adoption

The Foundling Hospital – UCD Cultural Heritage Collections

ucdculturalheritagecollections.com

Denny (Fitzmaurice), Lady Arabella, dictionary of Irish Biography (dib.ie)

Frances Clarke

Professor Eamon de Valera Jnr-A hypocrite and baby thief at the heart of the Irish establishment

Fergus Finlay, Irish Examiner 9th March 2021

The Embryo Project Encyclopaedia-Casti Connubi (1930), by Pope Pius XI

Katherine Brind 'Amour', published 20/01/20

The Mother and Child Scheme-The role of Church and State

Rhona McCord, The Irish Story (Irish History Online) 19/06/2013

Gaffney, Gertrude ('Gertie',Conor Galway) dictionary of Irish Biography (dib.ie)

Patrick Maume

Discovering Women in Irish History-The Women's Liberation Movement (scoilnet.ie) p.119

She was right: How Catherine Corless uncovered what happened in Tuam

The Journal.ie 03/03/2017

Final Report of the Commission of Investigation into Mother and Baby Homes

gov.ie 12/01/21

Adoption-Related Trauma and Moral Injury

Mirah Riben Huff Post, 27/06/2016.

Report on illegal adoptions recommends State inquiry (rte.ie) p

Aoife Hegarty-RTE Investigates 14/03/2022.

Authority admits thousands of adoptions illegal.

Claire O'Sullivan and *Conall O Fatharta*-Irish Examiner 07/07.2014

Church 'more complicit than most' in mother and baby scandal-
Sarah Burns Irish Times 16/01/2021.

'Lost' recordings of mother and baby home survivors retrieved.
Brendan Palenque Kelly, Sunday World 24/02/ 2021

Catholic Church in Ireland covered up child abuse.
The Guardian online (Associated Press), 26/11/2009

Church Insurance Covers Sex Abuse Claims,

Patsy McGarry, Religious Affairs Correspondent, Irish Times 05/02/03

Canada: 751 unmarked graves found at residential school
BBC News 24/06/2021

'They knew it and they let it happen', Uncovering Child Abuse in the Catholic Church

Spotlight 2002: *Joseph P. Kahn and Mike Damiano updated 22/09/2021*

Zappone reveals at least 126 children were wrongly registered as biological children of adoptive parents.

The journal.ie 29/05/2018

Government approves publication of the annual report of the Special Rapporteur on Child Protection, Professor Conor O'Mahony

gov.ie 28/01/2022